Praise for *The High Beings of Hawaii*
Encounters with Mystical Ancestors

*"Tanis offers our Hawaiian ancestors the opportunity
to speak to more people through her experiences
with them and does this with **humor and honor** and
captures their essence in her story."*

mahalo ke akua

mahalo na amakua

mahalo na kupuna o kahiko

me kealohapumehana

*which means "Thanking the gods, thanking the
ancestors, thanking the family ancestors from the old
time with love and warm aloha."*

—Kimokeo Kapahulehua,
founder of Kimokeo Foundation preserving Native Hawaiian Culture

*"A mystic and great storyteller, Tanis Helliwell details
the various types of ancestors, both physical and
spiritual, and how we are related to them. In describing
her adventures on the Hawaiian Islands she captures
the essence of what spiritual ancestors are all about.
She weaves fascinating and enchanting tales of how she
met the various old ones that reside there. You'll be
charmed and entertained as you read this book."*

—Dr. Steven Farmer,
author of *Healing Ancestral Karma* and *Earth Magic*.

*"Tanis continues to excite those who seek to challenge the margins of space and time. In **The High Beings of Hawaii**, she boldly ventures into the mystical realms to enlighten and inspire. It's a wonderful journey of heart, spirit and mind. An absorbing read of a different kind."*

—Barry Brailsford MBE MA (Hons),
historian and author of fifteen books including *Song of Waitaha, Song of the Stone, Song of the Old Tides, Wisdom of the Four Winds*

*"The word ancestor is quite a broad term that indigenous people understand well. We Westerners don't really grasp what ancestor means, and when we finally do, it opens our minds and hearts to great helpers we can use ... and they like to be used and acknowledged for they have a mighty task to do. Our earth would be a sorry place without their assistance. I highly recommend **The High Beings of Hawaii** to everyone interested in understanding the earth and its multi-dimensional living beings upon it."*

—Alice Friend,
artist, musician and shaman

THE
HIGH BEINGS
OF HAWAII

Also by Tanis Helliwell

BOOKS:

- *Hybrids: So you think you are human*
- *Summer with the Leprechauns: the authorized edition*
- *Pilgrimage with the Leprechauns: a true story of a mystical tour of Ireland*
- *Decoding Your Destiny: keys to humanity's spiritual transformation*
- *Manifest Your Soul's Purpose*
- *Take Your Soul to Work*
- *Embraced by Love*

DVDs

1. *Elementals and Nature Spirits*
2. *Hybrids: So you think you are human*
3. *Spiritual Transformation: Journey of Co-creation*

CDs

Series A — *Personal Growth Collection: Two Visualizations*

1. *Path of Your Life / Your Favorite Place*
2. *Eliminating Negativity / Purpose of Your Life*
3. *Linking Up World Servers / Healing the Earth*

Series B — *Inner Mysteries Collection: Talk and Visualization*

1. *The Celtic Mysteries / Quest for the Holy Grail*
2. *The Egyptian Mysteries / Initiation in the Pyramid of Giza*
3. *The Greek Mysteries / Your Male and Female Archetypes*
4. *The Christian Mysteries / Jesus' Life: A Story of Initiation*
5. *Address from The Earth/ Manifesting Peace on Earth*

Series C – *The Self-Healing Series: Talk and Visualization*

1. *The Body Elemental / Healing with the Body Elemental*
2. *Rise of the Unconscious / Encountering Your Shadow*
3. *Reawakening Ancestral Memory / Between the Worlds*

TANIS HELLIWELL

THE
HIGH BEINGS
OF HAWAII

ENCOUNTERS WITH
MYSTICAL ANCESTORS

Library and Archives Canada Cataloguing in Publication
Title: The High Beings of Hawaii: Encounters with Mystical Ancestors / Tanis Helliwell.
Names: Helliwell, Tanis, author. Description: Includes bibliographical references and
index. Identifiers: Canadiana (print) 20190042192 | Canadiana (ebook) 20190042249 |
ISBN 9781987831146 (softcover) | ISBN 9781987831160 (ebook)
Subjects: LCSH: Menehune—Hawaii. | LCSH: Shamanism. | LCSH: Spirits.
Classification: LCC GR110.H38 H45 2019 | DDC 398.209969—dc23

Helliwell, Tanis, author
The High Beings of Hawaii: encounters with mystical ancestors / Tanis Helliwell

ISBN 978-1-987831-14-6

Cover by Janet Rouss and NeueErde
Book design Janet Rouss

Published by Wayshower Enterprises
www.iitransform.com

Thank you
to the Ancestors
mahalo nui loa

Contents

Introduction

This book is about ancestors; not only our biological ancestors, but also spiritual ancestors that exist in higher realms and send us important messages if we are open to receive them. In these last decades, there has been increasing interest in beings from other realms, as shown by books, films and documentaries on angels, UFOs, faeries, ancestors. When we open to the possibility that other realms exist that are peopled by such beings, the door opens for us to experience these realms for ourselves. This is now occurring in our world.

Some individuals are crossing the bridge into this unseen world through their interest in finding biological ancestors, as seen by the immense popularity of websites on ancestry and genealogy. Their curiosity may stem from a desire to know more about themselves and the generations of relatives that created them. Why? Because in the western world we have become rootless. No longer living in the same place as our forbearers, raised by single parents and broken families, we desperately seek our roots.

At the same time, in our third-dimensional, physical reality the increase in interracial marriage, gay, surrogate and adoptive parents is expanding our idea of family and stretching us to think in terms of a global, not only a biological, family tree. Not only that. Scientific discoveries also play a huge part in redefining who our ancestors are. Through discovering that humans have interbred with Neanderthals, we are pressed to extend our idea of even what a human is.

As these realities increasingly become the norm of our society, I believe our next step in our evolution is to consider the non-visible, higher realms of ancestors and their relationship to us. This is the journey that *The High Beings of Hawaii: Encounters with Mystical Ancestors* takes you on and, I hope, in the form of an amusing story.

A journey to meet the ancestors often requires a guide. Dante had Virgil to guide him through the heavenly realms. I have a leprechaun. A Divine Comedy, indeed! Let me introduce you.

I first met Lloyd, as the "The Man" calls himself, over 20 years ago in a remote part of Ireland, in an old cottage well known for being "haunted by faeries." Lloyd is a member of a group of elementals—the race to which gnomes, elves, faeries and leprechauns belong—and this group is committed to working with humans to co-create a beautiful Earth together, one in harmony with natural and spiritual laws. Lloyd asked me to write *Summer with the Leprechauns* about our experiences so that more humans would join them in this great undertaking. Since then, he has encouraged me to meet elementals and other "unseen" beings of diverse races around the world and record what they wish humans to know about them.

In case, I am stretching your believability, I assure you that I drive a car, pay taxes and have facilitated both spiritual and corporate workshops internationally for over 30 years, however I am also a mystic. You may wonder what that means as it's a vague term many people use these days. Some people sing or dance well, play tennis, or are good on computers—none of my talents by the way. In my case, being a mystic means that I can see and hear beings in other realms that most folks are unaware of. Although I have had this "gift" since childhood, this quality can be developed and it's my life's work to teach others how to do this.

It's wonderful to witness that when you and I open to the possibility that other realms exist that are peopled by elementals, angels, and ancestors, Spirit opens the doors for us to experience these realms for ourselves. We travel more freely in the higher frequencies of the astral world and synchronicities increase, which gives clarity about our destiny and what our unique contribution is to the web of life.

An important door to another realm opened for me on my Hawaiian vacation when my leprechaun friend unexpectedly appeared and introduced me to the menehune (commonly believed to be the elementals of Hawaii), and to the mysterious dragon-like beings of legend, the mo'o. These beings are as real as you and I and live in realms we are destined to know in the very near future. They asked me to write this account, really an invitation, to awaken a connection to your biological and spiritual ancestors, and to impress on you, as they did on me, that the ancestors are always with you, helping and guiding. Of course, with an amusing leprechaun as a guide you can imagine that the story is anything but predictable. I invite you to join me on my topsy-turvy "vacation" to meet Lloyd, the menehune, and the mo'o—and to meet these ancient ancestors yourself.

"The ordinary astral universe ... is peopled with millions of astral beings who have come, more or less recently, from the Earth, and also with myriads of fairies, mermaids, fishes, animals, goblins, gnomes, demigods and spirits, all residing in different astral planets in accordance with karmic qualifications."

as told to Paramahansa Yogananda by his resurrected
Master Sri Yukteswar in *Autobiography of a Yogi*

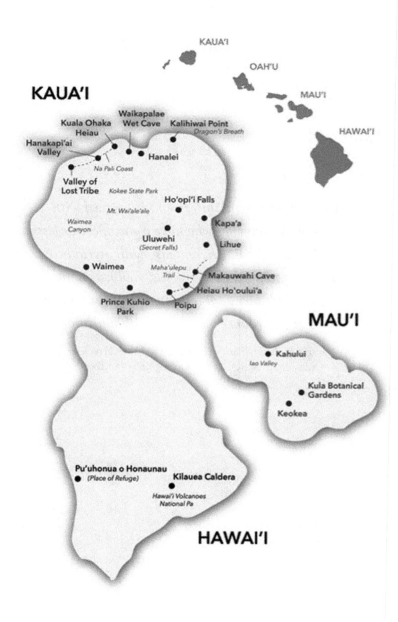

PART 1

Meeting Mythical Beings
in their Ancestral Land

If you live in Canada, as I do, winters can be cold and dreary. This is why, like many other snowbirds, I love to go to any sunny haven to escape. The Hawaiian Islands are my first choice and of these, Kauai, which is known by Hawaiians as the most spiritual island, is my favorite. It had been a busy year without a vacation, and recovering from a car accident, publishing a new book, running a spiritual organization, as well as facing the daily demands of life had plumb exhausted me. Having two weeks free in January, I looked for an available condo and, to my joy, discovered a cancellation on the south coast—the sunny part—of Kauai.

My partner Simon and I had only been there a few days, just long enough to get over jet lag, buy groceries, and unpack our swimsuits, when our plans were hijacked. I was lounging on the lanai, sipping my morning Earl Grey, and perusing brochures of fun things to do. The birds were chirping, the ocean was beckoning, and all was right in the world when Lloyd, my leprechaun friend, materialized in the beach chair across from me.

Lloyd is tall for a leprechaun, about four feet. This day he had bare feet and was wearing green shorts (his favorite color) and a bright Hawaiian shirt full of moving fish and flowers. Yes, I said moving. Lloyd, like all elementals, is way ahead of humans in his ability to manifest, so the fish on his shirt were swimming and the flowers were swaying, gifting me with the sweet fragrance of frangipane.

"Now that you've had your vacation, I'd like to introduce you to the menehune and another group," he said, crossing his hands on his rotund tummy.

Tearing my eyes away from his hypnotic shirt, I countered, "Hold on a minute. I haven't 'had' my vacation and am not intending to work on my holiday."

"When was it ever 'work' being with me?" my friend asserted, raising his left eyebrow.

"Point taken. However, every time I have the privilege of meeting your friends, you want me to write a book about it and that is work." I said, gazing intently at my brochures.

"Point taken," he laughed. "I'm here for a vacation, too, plus a bit of study, and I can promise you lots of interesting experiences. So what d'ya say?"

"Umm. Perhaps a little more information would help. The menehune are the elementals (Lloyd's preferred word for nature spirits) in Hawaii, aren't they?" I replied, taking a nonchalant sip of tea.

"That's what people say, however the story is more complex than that. And it's important to have no preconceptions about menehune. The other group I want you to meet are very special and powerful, and have few interactions with humans.

"What group would that be?" I nibbled at the bait he was dangling.

"Not so fast," Lloyd replied, reeling in the line. "I want you to have an open mind when you meet this group."

"As long as my vacation is still on, I wouldn't mind joining you… but only if it's fun."

Ukuleles echoed in the background, softening me. "No worries, I could use a holiday meself," Lloyd assured me, landing the fish.

He leaned forward, a charming grin on his face. "The only place to start is the sacred Wailua Valley, known as the ancient pathway of the Gods to the humans who first settled on the Hawaiian Islands. We'll paddle up the Wailua River, called the River of Dreams. I'll see you there tomorrow. Bright and early."

With these parting words, he disappeared, leaving me, as usual, to arrange all the details. Glancing down at my brochures I saw that, coincidentally, the one on top was for a kayak trip up the Wailua River. I decided to go and was sure that Simon, an ardent sailor and boater, would be keen to join me.

The next day at 7:00 a.m., shivering with the early morning cold, Simon and I made our way to the river. Simon is a good-humored, tall, hero-type, at least that's how he appears to me, but then I'm only up to his armpit. A slender, dreadlocked young guide, Paul, greeted us along with another couple ready for the river adventure. Taking charge, Simon signaled me to get in the front, while he leapt into the back of the kayak to start our trek. Living beside an ocean, we've kayaked often, so we paddled ahead of the other couple as Paul was instructing them.

Paddling silently through the hazy dawn, enjoying the stillness, I looked up to my left and saw the peak of a mountain breaking through the mist. The mountain observed our progress and from time to time I heard the water drip from our paddles as we glided through the glassy water. Suddenly Lloyd appeared, perched cross-legged in the bow of our kayak. Simon is a practical man, more interested in engines and sailing than leprechauns, so he doesn't see Lloyd. Fortunately, he's been privy to enough magical happenings with me that his belief in elementals and other "unseen" beings is not in question.

Lloyd (no paddling for him) sat regally erect. Gone was his Hawaiian shirt, replaced by his Irish Sunday best: a tight-fitting green jacket with brass buttons, black short pants, wool socks and heavy clogs. Beads of sweat rolled down his chubby cheeks. He stared at the shore and, following his gaze, I became aware of large numbers of small, slender human-like beings lining the shore. A delegation of dugout canoes launched from the bank and, paddling closer, I saw they were unlike any elementals I had met in the past. Hawaiians had described menehune to me as brown-skinned, two- to three-foot high, child-like beings. These beings were not them.

Seated in their dugouts, it was difficult to say exactly, but my best guess was they were almost human sized with long, thin arms and legs ... somewhat like a goblin. Their skin was a khaki color and, although they had two eyes, a nose and mouth, they more nearly resembled a human face crossed with a reptile. They were all males; naked, except for a bark-like loincloth and leis circling their necks.

My anxiety rose the closer they got as their non-human features became increasingly obvious. Catching up with our kayak presented no problem for them and they soon reached us. The male in the lead dugout approached Lloyd and bowed to him. When Lloyd bowed in return, the being extended his thin arms and placed a lei around my friend's neck. That male withdrew and others came forward to add their leis, until the leprechaun's breathing was threatened from an overabundance of welcome.

The first male grabbed the side of our kayak and moved closer to me. His smile revealed pointed teeth, so I remained rock still when he extended his olive-skinned arms and encircled my neck with a multi-colored lei.

Addressing me as the *wahine* (woman) who accompanies Lloyd, he said, "We are giving you flowers of rainbow colors, because we're honoring you as a teacher of many traditions."

"Thank you," I murmured, while attempting to erase prejudicial thoughts about his looks and open my heart more fully to his welcome.

Beings in higher dimensions communicate telepathically so I know he had heard my first thoughts, but he courteously ignored my bad manners. "See Mount Wai'ale'ale who looks down on us, blessing us with her waters," he said. "This is why we've always lived in this valley, and this is the place where the first humans came. We lived apart from them for a long while, but they knew about us, and we shared our knowledge with them. Later, some of us interbred with humans, but that's a story for another time."

I was intrigued to hear the story then, not at a later time, but he ignored this thought as well. "We're not menehune," he continued, "which I see in your mind that you were expecting; we are their guardians and teachers. We call ourselves mo'okane and we're descended from an older race Hawaiians refer to as mo'o."

At this point he looked up, and noticing our guide Paul and the other couple gaining on us, nodded a quick goodbye and pushed away from our kayak. Our human companions soon caught up and we resumed paddling. Meeting the moʻokane unsettled me and I sent Lloyd several telepathic prods for answers. Choosing to ignore them, he kept his eyes pointed forward.

Before long we came to a place where the channel narrowed. "Pull out there," Paul said, as he signaled us to land on a sandy beach under the canopy of an ancient rainforest.

Trying not to upset the kayak, I shakily managed to haul myself onto the land. After we pulled out of the water, Paul's next instructions were "Start walking", as he headed into the jungle.

Within moments, we encountered our first obstacle—a fast moving stream with no bridge. Paul grabbed a hanging rope and leapt into the water. I was walking behind him so was expected to go next. No way was I taking off my shoes and exposing my tender feet to the sharp things I was convinced resided at the bottom. Reluctantly, I eased myself into the cold stream and, hoping not to lose my footing, followed at a much slower pace. Elementals the world over, to which I now added another type of being—the moʻokane—often present little tests for humans who wish to meet them. This obstacle was just one in a long list of challenges I'd experienced over the years.

Although Lloyd could have skipped this part and teleported himself (a nice talent elementals have) to our final destination, he followed in our steps through the stream. Given that he was a foot shorter than me and weighed down by all those leis, he now found himself pushing through rushing water up to his chest. Clutching the rope with both hands to keep from being swept away, he grimaced while struggling to the opposite shore. The reptile-featured mo'okane lined the banks and observed his progress in silence. By his actions, I understood that Lloyd wanted to undergo the same challenges as the humans to show respect for the local inhabitants.

With step one successful, I sloshed in wet shoes along the forest trail into the valley where the ancient Hawaiian royalty had lived. The path took us over rocks, washed out slopes, and through numerous watercourses caused by the abundance of rain for which Kauai is famous. We hadn't gone far when our path emerged in the middle of an ancient Hawaiian temple, a *heiau*. Only volcanic stones from the original foundation were in evidence, but ancient religion and present day Hawaiians claim that the *mana* (life force) of the *'aina* (land) still exists there today.

I glanced around and saw extensive ruins of more temples, terraces, and habitations of the royal Hawaiians who originally had lived there. A deep hush surrounded us and I felt the presence of unseen ancestors. I paused to meditate and see if these beings wished to contact me. Time passes quickly in this state and when I opened my eyes, our guide had already left with the others. I hurried to catch up before I lost my way.

They were waiting for me where several immense boulders blocked the path. Paul started to scramble up, around, and over the rocks weaving a way so quickly that he must have known the route well from former treks. The rest of us followed tentatively, but follow we did. And it was well worth it when we emerged on the other side at our final destination: Uluwehi, the secret falls.

A few Hawaiian teenagers stood in the shallow end of the sacred pool, while one was swimming. Muddy and never one to shirk a good swim, I removed my shoes and waded in up to my knees, then quickly waded out again. Living north of Vancouver, I'm used to cool waters, but this was cold beyond what I was prepared for that day.

Glancing across the pool to the far cliff, I looked at the lovely 120' waterfall. It was dainty as waterfalls go and the cascading water created lacey patterns that revealed the rocks behind. As I took a photo of the serene setting, a faint rainbow began to form in the waterfall growing until it covered the entire cliff. Mesmerized, I watched a gigantic light being appear inside the rainbow. I immediately tuned in to what she wished to say. I say "she", because this rainbow being felt like a female.

"You would call me a water deva, although I have many names that will be better understood by you later," she said. "I guard this sacred area along with the menehune and mo'okane. A rainbow is made up of all colors and frequencies needed to manifest Spirit in this world. It's also a symbol of peace. I appear to you in this rainbow form, to acknowledge the name 'Singing Rainbows' that you were given long ago by a Cherokee medicine man. Your path is to link all traditions of the world together in peace, just as my path is to bless humans who come here and give them peace and joy—two qualities in short supply in your world."

As the deva spoke, the rainbow grew in power and clarity, and I remained transfixed. It was clear she was speaking only with me because the swimmers in the pool were totally unaware of what was happening.

"On your way here, you met the ones we call the mo'okane. Mo'okane are a sub-race of the mo'o—water dragons known to the Hawaiians in their myths. Their purpose was to be servants for humans. Servant means helper to us...to align humans to both Spirit and nature. The mo'okane—the name for the mo'o who choose to take a human-like form—are related to the great creator god Kane. Kane is one of the main Hawaiian gods and he created the moʻo before the menehune or humans. Both the moʻo and moʻokane are our medicine people, guardians of the Earth, and they have gifts of healing to share with you and your leprechaun partner."

"Why are you and they speaking with me?" I inquired as respectfully as I could. This trek was becoming more complicated than I anticipated…certainly more than the leprechaun had led me to believe.

The water deva paused and I felt her shift her attention to my right where many moʻokane and Lloyd stood observing our conversation. Referring to the moʻokane who had gifted me with the lei in the kayak, she said, "The moʻokane will speak for themselves."

"We are shape-shifters descended from moʻo, who are most commonly seen as female 12- to 30-foot dragon-like beings. The second reason we call ourselves moʻokane is that the word "kāne" in this context means "male/man" and we wanted to experience male as well as female bodies like the moʻo. We moʻokane decided to take a human-like shape so that we could walk more easily on the land and experience both male and female bodies. We find this easier to converse with you and our young friend," said the moʻokane, staring at Lloyd whose face was barely poking out above the leis.

Turning back to me, the moʻokane continued, "Moʻo figure in the oldest Hawaiian stories and are a key to its mystical past. In other nations, we would be called water dragons and we have the gifts of long-life, wisdom, deep seeing and some would say possessiveness of places and people we protect. We are guardians of water, rivers, ponds, and freshwater sources, and Hawaiians have worshipped us from early times as ancestral gods. For many reasons our paths diverged from those of humans and many no longer believe in us. This is one reason we decided to take a human shape and why we have contacted you to tell our story."

An appeal to my sympathy is my weak area. Visions of an evaporating holiday were crossing my mind, so I was not going to agree without a good reason. "Wouldn't it be better for you to tell your story to a Hawaiian? Some of them must be able to see and speak with you and they'd have more credibility than a Canadian who knows, let me add, nothing about you."

"Well, that brings us to our second reason for contacting you," the mo'okane responded, smiling his sharp-toothed smile. "The fact that you consciously know nothing about us adds to your credibility in telling the story. You know more than you are aware and we wish to reawaken a relationship with us that is sleeping in your subconscious. In fact, our mission is much broader than that; we want to re-awaken ALL people to the sleeping levels of their subconscious."

Becoming increasingly concerned about these hints of relationship with khaki-colored, shape-shifting dragons, I turned to Lloyd for support. He refused to meet my eyes and stood united with the mo'okane. Some friend. At that exact moment, other beings appeared. If they had been there all along, I hadn't seen them. Had they just arrived? Being flustered, I could not tell.

The mo'okane gestured towards them. "These beings are royal menehune, who we speak of as *ali'i*. Hawaiians, humans that is, called their royal class ali'i in the old days too. You now know who taught them this term, don't you?"

These royal menehune were brown-skinned and lacked the reptilian facial features of the mo'okane and so, to my eyes, were more human-like. The menehune ali'i wore leis around their necks and in their hair, and were taller than me by a long shot. I assumed one middle-aged male was the leader, because he was wearing more leis. His wooden staff was carved with images of beings and plants that I surmised represented his family's totems. He and the other menehune ali'i seemed content to be seen by me, however, none of them spoke. Respectful and attentive, they seemed to be witnessing my interaction with the mo'okane.

My Gawd! First I get mo'okane, or was that mo'o, who want me to tell their story and now they throw in another group that won't talk to me. And Lloyd is no help at all. Hearing my thoughts, the rainbow being in the sacred waterfall appeared to take pity.

"The menehune ali'i who dwell here seldom interact with humans," she said. "They hold to the traditional ways, and do not wish to dilute who they are by interaction with modern humans. This is not a slight on you, but a way for them to preserve themselves and their traditions. These are the royal caste of menehune, the rulers, the ali'i. They were attracted to the early Hawaiians who came to this valley and taught them our ways. This valley, then, became home to the royal Hawaiians who were respectful of our menehune traditions. Over time some royal menehune and royal Hawaiians interbred, but they were asked to leave because the community did not feel this was a good idea. Now, the menehune ali'i in this valley mostly stay apart from humans."

I could see how the menehune ali'i could interbreed with humans because they looked similar, just as elves in Europe closely resemble humans and have interbred with them both in the past and present. Still there is something in the eyes of elementals and humans that show they come from different races, even as you can tell a wolf from a large dog. As I continued to observe the royal menehune, I saw among them smaller childlike ones.

Noticing this, the waterfall deva said, "These little ones are also menehune. They enjoy interacting with humans and are the ones most humans commonly see, so humans think that all menehune look like them. There are many kinds of menehune, including the royal ali'i who are similar to what you think of as royal elves. There are also menehune living in the forests who are more like forest elves. A third kind of menehune, similar to pixies, are the small menehune humans think are like children, but they are sometimes very old and fully grown.

"One more thing. This place is the east of the island of Kauai. We want you to go to the north, west, and south to meet the mo'okane and menehune in all these locations, since we are all different. Also, we would like you to visit our sister, Pele, the volcano goddess and deva of fire, but you must go to the Big Island for that."

She paused. "Put your hands in the water of my pool and wash your face and hair," she commanded. Having done as she had instructed, I looked up to see the brilliance of her rainbow increase tenfold until it covered the entire side of the pool. The water deva was outlined in a magnificent array of shimmering colors.

"Take another photograph," she urged, "so you can show visual proof of what you have seen today."

I did as she asked, although I did not need proof myself. I felt her bless my journey and was astounded that the people in the pool were unaware of what was occurring. Our guide Paul, however, was different. Staring at the rainbow, he walked over to me and said, "I've been coming to the pool for years and I've never seen anything like that."

I shared my pictures, which amazed him, and it was easy for me to see that Paul had elemental ancestry, although I didn't know if he'd understand me mentioning this. I ventured cautiously into that territory. "Paul," I said, "I've been talking to the deva in the falls about the menehune I've been seeing in this forest."

"I feel the presence of the menehune," he replied. "A friend of mine was camping here and saw a menehune across from the campfire. He said it was a few feet tall, brown-skinned, and looked like a child."

Paul was describing the little ones I'd seen, but I wondered what he knew of the mo'okane. "Do you know anything about those who are approximately five or six feet tall, greenish-skinned, with more reptilian faces...the ones who call themselves mo'okane?" I asked.

"I'm very interested in the ancient myths and unseen beings, but I don't know about mo'okane," he replied, making me wonder about what I was seeing. I was happy that he believed in menehune, and it was not the first time in my life that I had seen what others have not. But here, I was in unknown territory. Lloyd had pushed me into this experience. Would he help? I glanced over to where he still stood, a white face in a sea of chocolate and khaki. He and the others stood rapt in their own conversation with the water deva. It did not include me, so I turned away and started to walk back.

Teachings by Moʻokane in Kokee

The next day I was up early and found Lloyd sitting on the lanai enjoying deep breaths of fresh air and perusing the sky. "It'll be a clear day, not something you can depend on in Kauai, so you'd best head for Waimea Canyon…the top," he stated. "Very often it's shrouded in mist and we want you to be able to see it at its best."

"Just a moment," I asserted, "Don't forget I'm on vacation here. I want to know exactly what you have planned before we go any further."

He looked at me fixedly and said absolutely nothing, not one word.

"Well, is this how much help you're going to be?" By now I was really annoyed.

No response from Himself.

"Well, I'm thinking of not doing what you want. Simon and I can have a lovely time by ourselves. You're just lucky he's always been willing to go along with your suggestions…until now."

Lloyd sat there twiddling his plump thumbs with exaggerated patience. Finally he said, "It's not that I don't want to talk with you, it's that I cannot. You're just going to have to trust me on this."

I softened slightly, but was not ready to agree to an all-for-him/ nothing-for-me deal. Sensing this, he cast pleading eyes towards me that I couldn't resist.

"Could we at least talk about the moʻokane? I've never heard anything about them before and would like some confirmation."

"You humans. Unbelievable. You have these wondrous meetings and what do you do? Doubt, that's what! It's a miracle that the moʻokane even took the time to meet with you."

Although Lloyd pretended annoyance, his eyes twinkled. He never missed a chance to take a dig at what he regards as a totally stupid attitude of humans—to always want proof for everything we see, hear, or feel.

"Just a few words," I said, and added, "Not only that…"

"No. First have your own experiences at the top of the mountain. We'll talk later…maybe," he added. "I'm going to wean you off this proof thing."

Conceding defeat (brother, was he stubborn), I changed my tack, "Waimea Canyon is one of the 'must sees' so Simon and I were planning to go there anyway. You seem very keen that we go today. Will you be our travel guide, or do you have other plans?"

"I'll join up once you get to the top trail and, just maybe, others will be there as well," he smiled, fading ever so slowly from the feet up… just one more thing elementals can do that humans cannot. His clear message.

A few hours later, not to be hurried, Simon and I were chugging up the road overlooking Waimea Canyon. Simon is a frugal type and our car was the most economical model available, so I had doubts if we would make it to the vague location Lloyd had stipulated. About three-quarters of the way, we pulled into a ranger station to check our bearings. After all, we had no map and were going on you-know-who's instructions. A fit, middle-aged woman ranger was giving hiking maps to interested hikers, so I got in line.

When my turn came, pointing to the map, I asked, "Could you show me the last trail at the top?"

"That's Kaluapuhi Trail in Kokee State Park," she answered and then added, "Menehune are known to frequent that trail." That was all the confirmation I needed.

The park, located in a cloud forest, lies on the western edge of the Alaka'i plateau, the remnant of a six million-year-old volcanic caldera. Directly before the end of the road, there is one last forest path, the Kaluapuhi Trail. Parking the car at the beginning of the trail, I opened the door to a cool breeze. At elevations of 4,000 feet, the average temperature is 60 degrees, so we quickly donned sweaters and changed out of our shorts before setting out. When possible, I prefer to walk in silence to see and listen to birds, animals, and plants, as well as beings such as elementals, who live in other dimensions. Because of this, I often find it distracting to speak with others. Simon has long been respectful of my need for silence and walks ahead or behind, so I can enter a meditative state.

Surprisingly, it hadn't rained for over a week and the trail was dry…at least to start. We soon entered a pristine meadow surrounded by continually shifting rainbows dimly visible through the mist. Rare birds, found only on the Hawaiian Islands, called their fellows warning of our advance. Although the park service clears the trail of invasive species to keep the area as natural as possible, naughty blackberries, which had escaped the clearing, co-existed beside local blooming kahili ginger.

Thank heavens the park service is clearing away invasive species as 90 percent of Hawaii's native plants grow nowhere else. Because a new plant arrives naturally on the average of only once every 35,000 years, they are precious indeed and have evolved over hundreds of millennia into very diverse species. Unfortunately, today over 25 percent of endangered species of the United States are from Hawaii, therefore it was a gift to enjoy this special place and I was grateful for the leprechaun's urging.

He must have picked up my thoughts as "The Man" joined us at that moment. Dressed according to a local outfitter magazine, Lloyd had on oversized hiking boots—his feet were not diminutive—and carried an immense backpack. He tramped silently ahead. Taking his cue, I remained quiet and enjoyed the walk, content to let the hike be only a hike. As we meandered deeper into the forest, the path, although still beautiful, grew increasingly muddy.

My leprechaun friend seemed preoccupied and marched on with head down. Around a bend in the path, I glimpsed a group of mo'okane off to the left in a denser part of the forest. They were hard to keep in sight as with their khaki-colored skin they blended so well with the forest vegetation. Several were cloaked with headdresses of brilliant bird feathers. Thinking that Lloyd and I were both invited, I moved to join them, only to be greeted by a STOP look on their grim faces.

Lloyd took a moment to say, "They've been planning a ritual just for me today. And," he added, shrugging his pack, "I've brought gifts for them, too." With these words, he headed for the gathering.

I didn't know if I should feel left out or relieved. In any case, I was curious. I saw an olive-skinned reptilian-faced mo'okane dressed in a loincloth, grinding a root in a large, stone bowl with what looked like a volcanic stone implement. When the root was thoroughly ground, a second one spat into the compound and started adding water. The liquid was a brownish color and I recognized that it was the root of the kava plant that Hawaiians call *ʻawa*, used for social occasions and in ceremonies. ʻAwa is renowned for its healing properties for anxiety. It calms those who drink the liquid while keeping them mentally alert. It is a sacred plant and quite an honor for Lloyd to be invited to join the ceremony.

A few tall, royal menehune aliʻi kept apart from the others and I could have sworn they were the same ones I'd observed at the waterfall. They didn't interact with Lloyd, but gave the impression of witnessing the ritual. Noticing me studying them, they turned not unfriendly faces towards me. I retreated to the path and sensed their permission to observe the first part of the ritual.

From that vantage point, I witnessed one moʻokane place a green lei with red puff-ballish *ʻohia lehua* blossoms around Lloyd's neck, while an older one held out a smaller lei apparently meant for his head. Lloyd ALWAYS wears a hat and I could see that, lei or no lei, he was averse to removing it. The older one waited patiently. Reluctantly Lloyd complied, revealing his shortage of hair. His vanity was a small price to pay, as I realized these beings regarded him as royalty and wanted to honor him. My insight was confirmed when the second moʻokane, addressed my friend as "The Grand" (the title leprechauns call their chief), and placed the crown of native flowers on Lloyd's head.

Other beings poured some of the kava drink on the ground. I overheard them offer the ʻawa as a blessing to Laka, the goddess of the woods and patroness of vegetation. Only after the moʻokane had observed that ritual did they proceed to offer some of the ʻawa to

Lloyd. From the path, I heard them welcome him as an ambassador working with humans to help heal the Earth. Lloyd wasn't one to turn down a new kind of beverage, especially if it was mood enhancing, so he looked eager to participate in that part of the ritual.

All too soon, the regal menehune aliʻi, looking my way, sent me a message to move on. Reciprocating with a non-invasive "thank you" towards the celebrants, I commenced my journey along the trail. Within 15 minutes, the path came to a junction. The path to the left said "Dead End" and, a gate detered walkers from entering. Although drawn in that direction, I felt urged by unseen beings to continue further along the trail. So I did… and followed it down and down, with no end to the descent in sight. Turning around, huffing and puffing, I retraced my steps back up. Returning to the "Dead End" gate, I sensed that the way was no longer energetically closed. On the contrary: I was invited to enter. It was almost as if the gate had opened towards a tunnel of light.

I proceeded respectfully into a tunnel and soon came to a grove of large Japanese cedar trees where a group of moʻokane and royal menehune aliʻi and child-like ones stood. They resembled the beings I'd met at the secret fall, however, instead of carrying a carved walking stick, a koʻokoʻo, the adults carried spears.

One of the older reptilian-faced moʻokane stepped forward to speak with me. I thought he must be the leader of the moʻokane because his spear had more carvings than the others. Otherwise I couldn't have determined his status. His eyes had the yellowish cast of a snake and his faint skin markings reminded me of scales. The word "dragon" came to mind which conjured thoughts of wisdom and fierce intelligence, while images of the beneficent oriental dragon collided with the evil dragon of the western world.

Once again, I struggled to reserve judgment as none of his actions appeared menacing.

"We live in the mountains," he said. "We broke away from the menehune that settled in the Wailua River Valley when the second wave of larger Hawaiians came from Tahiti. To keep our culture pure, we withdrew into remote, wild places such as here. We learned to hunt the smaller wild pig that the first Hawaiians brought. The much larger European pigs were brought later, and now we hunt a cross-breed."

I was intrigued by this information. Most nature beings I've met, trolls excluded, tend towards vegetarianism. Abruptly, a new thought crossed my mind. "Were these moʻokane and menehune even nature spirits?"

The moʻokane elder totally ignored my wandering mind and continued, "These pigs are our enemies, because they tear up our habitations, and dig up and eat plants that we cultivate. In the Polynesian Islands, you humans are known as 'long pigs' and we think of you as being a kind of pig. You come into our forest, take our trees, bring in invasive plants, and pollute our air with fuel from your cars. And you are so noisy, there is no silence around you."

I agreed with his scathing assessment, but then returned an obvious question: "Then why do you wish to communicate with me? I am a human after all."

He replied, "You're interested in healing the Earth and all beings and we want you to share our message with others to catalyze their own experiences so we can speak directly to them. Also, we're your ʻaumakua. You would say ancestor. You have lived on these islands. You don't understand all that means right now, but you will before your journey ends."

I was immensely curious to know how a dragon-like shape changer could be my ancestor but knew from his don't ask expression that I wasn't going to receive more clarification at that moment. With nothing to lose, I asked another question. "Why don't the royal menehune ali'i speak with me?"

The ali'i stood immobile and erect, ignoring me while the mo'okane replied. "In Hawaiian terms, you are more a *kahuna pule*, a priest or shaman, or a *kahuna lapa'au*, a medicine person, than one of the ali'i. It's taboo, *kapu*, for ali'i of either menehune or humans to speak with you. The menehune ali'i don't communicate directly with Lloyd either, as he is contaminated from working with humans. Presently, there is nothing you can do about this and our menehune ali'i will witness what we, the mo'okane, say to you. You see, we mo'okane, like you, are shaman so we can speak with you."

As he spoke, the child-like menehune played around my feet weaving ropes to trip me if I wasn't careful. They were enjoying their game; I obviously wasn't kapu to them. I could only take a moment to notice them, because the elder stiffened, making it clear he wished to have my attention.

"On Hawaii, we mo'okane have four main tribes: the river ones, mountain ones, beach dune dwellers, and the fourth is difficult to speak of, because you have no reference point for them. The fourth tribe—that you think of as devas—live in a subtler dimension than us. I'm speaking of devas of the wind and clouds and they are the strongest ones. We Hawaiians have over 200 names for wind because of its many qualities. For instance, *nuala* is a sudden shower and it's angry; *mikio* is strong and gusty; *malanai* is a gentle breeze; and *lulau* is a misty breeze."

I was tempted to ask something else, but his forbidding look stopped me. The elder must have read my mind because he began to address my thoughts.

"In our gatherings on the Hawaiian Islands, we decide how much to resist human encroachment, and how much to partner with you humans. Both menehune and mo'okane are partnering humans in the leprechaun's group," he said, stressing that it was Lloyd's group. "These individuals defend humans at our enclaves and want to have more contact with them. The menehune ali'i, however, are especially resistant to partnering with humans, because they fear that humans won't respect them and the old traditians. Their argument is that white humans in Hawaii, those we call *haole* (meaning foreigner), do not respect the Polynesian Hawaiians. And the Polynesian humans, when they came to our islands, did not respect the menehune either."

Feeling chastised, I wondered if he had drawn the short straw and was told to speak with me instead of his apparent favorite, Lloyd. He picked up that thought, too, because his face mellowed as he continued.

"Some mo'okane and menehune, along with elementals and races from other countries, have incarnated in your human world so they can help their races and all beings. Because of this, most of us want to support your work with hybrids of various races that have entered human evolution. This includes me," he revealed, before firming up again. "But we don't want to lose our traditions. We have a major request that we want you to convey to all humans. Respect our vegetation! Don't bring any more foreign species to our land, as we are having great difficulty maintaining our local birds, vegetation, and trees."

With these last words, he clamped his mouth shut, crossed his spear in front of his chest, and stepped back into the group. Clearly, I was dismissed.

Simon had been wandering on his own, while I had been speaking to the ancestors. Although he does not see other realms himself, he is always supportive of me and gives me space for my encounters. We have both noticed over time that magical synchronicities continually happen in our lives when we do this. With perfect timing, he returned from his hike and we retraced our steps back the way we had come. The small child-like menehune followed at my heels chattering happily between themselves. I was listening to their babbling, which I could not understand, and as a result, I wasn't paying attention when I came upon a large muddy puddle over which a low branch hung. Struggling to avoid the puddle, my white hat caught on the branch and dropped into the mud. The small menehune thought this was hilarious and kept punching each other in their round little arms. I was fairly certain they were involved in tricking this human but it was all good-natured.

Having accomplished their mission, they allowed us to proceed unhindered along the path. Coming to the exit, Simon paused while I waited for inner guidance about what we should do next. Receiving a strong message to drive to the end of the road at Wai'ale'ale, we followed it.

At almost 4200 feet, Wai'ale'ale is known as the wettest place on Earth. Luckily, it was not raining, but we found ourselves in exceptionally damp clouds. A dense mist covered us in a powerful silence, and then passed by, leaving us in bright sunlight, before embracing us again. Magical rainbows glistened through the mist, triggering a strong memory of living in mists in early Lemuria.

Devas swirled in the clouds and rainbows and I suddenly realized these were the fourth tribe of moʻokane that the moʻokane elder had mentioned, making it even clearer to me that the moʻokane, like their ancestors the dragon-like moʻo, were shape-changers.

The devas moved closer as the mist enshrouded me again. "We've been here since this planet was first established," one of them said. "The Els, who came from Sirius in early times, created us by thought. That is what clouds are, but then again, you could say that everything is created by thought. The Els instructed us to condense mist to form more water on this planet and we are relatively unchanged since then. We don't call ourselves elementals, although we recognize that we are a kind of elemental as we create with the elements. We move between ether and the substance of your physical world."

"You remind me of beings in the mist who I met in New Zealand," I said.

"Few places still remain on Earth where we exist in the same realms as humans," the deva replied. "One of these is Lake Waikaremoana on the north island of New Zealand where the ancestors of elementals, the Tuatha de Danaan, have lived since Lemurian times."

With the deva's words, I recalled meeting these ancestors on Lake Waikaremoana. The homeland of the Tuhoe people, this lake is surrounded by native rainforest that's never been logged. A Tuhoe elder, Ragnamarie Pere, told me that old elementals wanted to speak with me and, to meet them, I'd have to walk around the lake by myself. Never one to say "no" to an invitation by elementals, I set off on a beautiful sunny day, which by the next morning had turned into a cyclone. I plodded through heavy winds and rain for four days and met similar beings to the Hawaiian deva. Recognition flooded me as the deva of the mist continued speaking.

"We are conscious. We have our own myths, stories, and reason for being. In Hinduism and the earlier Vedas we are referred to as 'devas'—lesser gods. In ancient Ireland they thought of us as the Sidhe, also known as the Tuatha de Danaan. As with elementals who are our descendants, there are many types of devas and we in the high mists of Kauai belong to the race of devas who create the water on Earth. Because we move water around the planet to grow all living beings, without us, there would be no earth, no fertility. Devas are half-divine beings, what in the Hawaiian culture is thought of as lesser gods, or ancestral guardians."

With these last words, the mist that had embraced me evaporated and the sun emerged. The consciousness that had spoken withdrew with the mist, leaving me to reflect on its teachings. I was aware that these Hawaiian ancestors were the same as others found elsewhere in the world by other names. How precious that we humans still have our myths to point the way to other realms.

Tired from a long day, I looked forward to speaking with Lloyd that evening about my encounters and to hear what had happened to him. Devoted as he seemed to breaking "The Human" of expectations and explanations, he was a no-show.

How Males and Females Differ

Before dawn Simon and I were catapulted out of sleep by the ever-present cocks crowing. Feral chickens on Kauai love to serenade humans day and night and, if it's not raining, I sleep outside under the stars, so I was serenaded more loudly than most.

Thinking we might as well take advantage of rising early to go for a cool walk, we headed for the Mahaʻulepu Heritage Trail that starts at Shipwreck Beach near Poipu. The walk is very scenic and parallels the ocean along sand dunes that are composed of limestone and sandstone pinnacles. The beginning of the trail was a bit heavy going as our feet continually sunk into the slippery sand. However we soon found a path along the limestone cliffs and walking became much easier from there. Following the path, we wandered into the trees and back out to the coast. Every view of the sea was breathtaking. Still, it was hot and I'd removed my sweater and stripped to a t-shirt by 9:00 a.m.

Although the beauty of the sand pinnacles and rugged coastline was reason enough to go, I had a secondary motivation. The deva at the waterfall had instructed me to seek out the moʻokane and menehune of the dunes and I was attempting to honor her request.

But they hadn't contacted me yet, and Lloyd was also absent—probably sleeping soundly after his "mood enhancing drink" the previous day. Happy to be left alone by unseen beings, I was enjoying my walk with Simon, when we came to a Hawaiian temple.

Heiau Hoʻouluiʻa is so ancient that its true name has been forgotten. Now called by its generic name, meaning "fishing temple", it's thought that long ago there were two grass huts here: One to give offerings to the god of the sea, and the second being the living quarters of the *kupuna*, or elderly person, who did the offerings.

Hawaiians feel strongly, and I concur, that it is essential to be respectful when entering any heiau, which are like churches used for sacred ceremonies. Therefore, we stuck to the path in order not to damage the site. Often I feel the presence of guardians when I'm near a heiau, or sacred sites in general, and I immediately saw the guardians of this heiau. They had committed to that role while alive and, now that they were dead, they fulfilled their function in the astral world. I felt no need to contact the guardians and usually think it's best to leave the dead in peace.

The temperature increased making it too hot for pale-skinned tourists who had neglected to bring water. Sweating profusely, we turned around and started back. About halfway, seeking shade from the blazing sun, I stopped for a breather in a grove of casuarina pine trees. Simon, having lived in Greece for many years, and lacking Irish blood, can take heat. He went to sit overlooking the water, where we had seen whales breaching earlier.

Sitting with my back against a tree, I closed my eyes to meditate and, when I opened them several minutes later, tattooed faces were staring at me. Darkened by the sun, and slender with bare feet and splayed toes, most were naked from the waist up and dressed only in loincloths made of dune grasses. Although many of the tattoos were similar, each individual's were unique. Some of them stood holding a koʻokoʻo whose point rested in the ground, and others had a spearhead on the end of their stick. The koʻokoʻo might have defined each member's role, depending on if they were warriors, kahuna (medicine people), or some other role. Having only spoken with males until now, I was surprised to see females among what seemed to be a purposeful group. Some were dressed similarly to the males and were naked to their waists, while others wore colorful print dresses to their ankles.

I found it interesting that the tall royal aliʻi and the small child-like menehune were absent in the group and were replaced by menehune that more closely resembled the moʻokane. The most noticeable difference being that the menehune tended to be rounder and the moʻokane leaner, which immediately got me wondering if the menehune and moʻokane were interbreeding and becoming hybrids like they reportedly had been doing with humans.

I didn't have time to investigate further as a grim moʻokane with the most tattoos greeted me with an astounded, "Where is Lloyd? We prepared a welcome for him…although we're happy to meet you as well." I felt a bit like a third wheel and was uncertain if it was because I was a human, a female, or for some other reason. More questions than answers were presenting themselves and as humans, myself included, like definite answers, I found not knowing uncomfortable.

I replied, "I don't know where he is, or if he's coming today. I last saw him when we met the menehune and moʻokane in Kokee."

I didn't mention that he'd been drinking ʻawa and who knows what else after I left. One tries to help a partner save face.

Speak of the devil! Lloyd made a startling entrance. Naked from the waist up, his furry, plump chest was tinged pink. Exposing white Irish skin to the Hawaiian sun seemed to have the same result for both elementals and humans. From the waist down, he wore a sarong composed of bunches of Irish shamrocks wilting in the heat and his bare feet looked endearingly tender exposed to the sharp grasses. The entire outfit demonstrated how, from head to toe, he was doing his best to fit in with local dress codes.

His sarong kept slipping over his ample belly and did not look well-secured. I wondered about what parts of his anatomy would be revealed if his shamrocks continued shriveling. Do Irish, like Scots, go unclad under their kilts? Lloyd picked up my thought and gave me a "mind your own business" look. He appeared unconcerned with the decreasing sarong, so why should I be worried.

Each of the menehune wore leis made out of shells. One of the male menehune carried one for Lloyd and a female had one for me. They stepped forward simultaneously to place these welcoming gifts around our necks. While looking me in the eye, the female pressed her nose and forehead to mine and shared my breath. This is called the *honi* by Hawaiians where two beings share the *hā*, the divine breath of life. It is a beautiful and sacred greeting and, as I reciprocated, my heart opened wide. After this, the stern moʻokane advanced with a cord made of dried plants. He signaled Lloyd and I to join hands and Lloyd nodded to me to do so.

I hesitated. I'd been dropped into a ceremony that no one told me about and for which I lacked any protocol. Sensing my distress, my friend smiled to reassure me and extended his right hand. When I took it in my left, the moʻokane nodded approval and quickly tied the cord around our joined hands.

"This is to signal the bond that humans have with us and the Earth," he said, turning to both of us as he spoke. "And this rope records the seriousness of the contract our people are making with humans."

"Some of our menehune and moʻokane already have human partners," he continued and, with his eyes boring into mine, he projected images of Hawaiian *kumu* who are experts and teachers in a craft and *kāhuna* who are the shaman. "Our community wants to partner with humans. We hope that by blending our energies with yours, you'll become better guardians of nature and all living beings. The community is very important to us and we have given great thought to the ones we are putting forward."

Good heavens! What exactly is happening here and why hasn't Lloyd prepared me. He, unlike me, seemed very aware of his role as he began to speak.

"It's important to realize that you cannot revoke your decision once you have committed. You should consider this for one turn of the sun. If you decide to become partners with a human, he or she will change you, not only for one life, but for all your lives. Are you certain you wish to do this?"

As he looked over the assembled group, it became clear from their eyes and body language that five of the candidates were terrified. They obviously didn't need "one turn of the sun" to make their decision and stepped back. Five young males, five young females, five middle-aged tattooed men, and one mature, taller, female menehune wearing an ankle-length muumuu remained. The young ones looked nervous and the older ones determined. Both groups were composed of a mixture of menehune and moʻokane.

"Are you ready to take your vows?" Lloyd asked.

The serious moʻokane, facilitating the ceremony, stepped forward and turned towards Lloyd. "The elders have prepared these ones for several years since hearing about your group. The older ones," he said, pointing to the middle-aged males and female, "have trained the younger ones to study humans as they walk through our dunes. They listen to human conversations to see what interests them. They do this to reduce the shock when they receive a human partner and to help them become a better partner. These individuals are ready to be tested by you."

The taller, mature female glanced at the moʻokane spokesman for permission to speak. He nodded approval. Talking to me and gesturing towards the five young females, she said, "These females request a female partner, if possible. They have many healing gifts and plant lore to enrich the life of any female and they hope their partner will share human female customs with them."

All eyes turned to me...the human. I chose my words with care. "If my leprechaun partner is willing to honor your request, I certainly am. It's advantageous to females of both our races to share knowledge as there are things we know that seem to be unknown to males."

With that, the females broke into laughter, which dispersed the tension that I'd felt in the gathering until then. Lloyd smiled and winked, his equivalent of a pat on the back.

Clearing his throat, as the laughter died down, he now stepped forward to begin his part in what I now understood to be an initiation ceremony. He spoke loudly to intensify the experience for each of the initiates.

"Are you committing to partner with a human when a suitable one is available?" he asked, solemnly scanning each face. They all nodded their acceptance. Walking from one to the next, he placed a hand on each of their foreheads to record their unique identity. He would hold their identities in memory for the time when the right human would appear. At such time, each initiate would be joined with a human.

Everyone looked grateful and proud to be doing something to benefit their community. Their stern leader, however, proceeded to scold me for being an hour late. "We were calling you to stop walking because we didn't want to interact with so many humans. The trails are busier when the sun rises."

"Get ready for that. Humans have problems hearing us when we want to get their attention," stated Lloyd, poking good-naturedly at me.

At a nod from the leader, one of his assistants blew a conch shell announcing the end of the ceremony, but surprisingly, the group didn't disperse. Instead, each individual, smiling and relaxed, walked towards Lloyd and me. The serious mo'okane unexpectedly softened and, leaning forward, touched his nose and forehead to mine. While sharing breaths, I felt his blessing for the work I do with elementals.

This seemed to be the social time, although I still had several questions brewing. Turning to the mature female who had spoken to me earlier, I said, "I'm interested to learn about the various tattoos that you and the others have. Is that a safe topic to discuss, because I have no wish to offend?"

"Come, let us women sit in the shade and I'll happily tell you," she answered signaling me to sit with her and the other females in a nearby grove of casurina pines. After we seated ourselves cross-legged in the sand, the males followed and clustered around us. They didn't speak and held a respectful silence and, by their attitude, I became aware that the mature female was revered by them. Still it was difficult to decide exactly what she was. One moment she resembled a tall, fuller-bodied menehune, another moment a human.

"You may call me Daisy," she began. I knew that she gave me a pseudonym, and probably for the same reason that Lloyd doesn't tell his real name. Both wish to remain inaccessible to curious humans who might want to call on them indiscriminately. Still, I understood it was her way of putting me at ease.

"As you see," she continued, pointing to both the males and females, "each of us have individual tattoos, *kakau* we call them, and our lives are recorded in our tattoos. Some kakau are for protection, while others mark important events in our lives—even our spiritual designation is recorded. Still other kakau, are for our family heritage and status in the community. Have you noticed that males tend to have more than females? This demonstrates their bravery, as it is a painful process to get a kakau.

"We only do kakau in black, unlike modern-day humans," she added with a look of reluctant acceptance. "Our skin is pierced with a sharp implement, perhaps a bird's beak or claw, and then a mixture of soot and ash is put in the cut.

"Males traditionally have kakau on their legs, arms, face, and body," Daisy explained, slowly indicating the location each male in the group had one. "We females usually have kakau on our hands, wrists, or even tongue," she added, opening her mouth to proudly show me her tattoo.

Fascinated by her explanation, I remembered how long ago I considered putting a small, colored butterfly tattoo on my buttock, but I hadn't acted on the urge for fear of it sagging in later years.

The females commenced laughing behind their hands. The males, on the other hand, tried to keep a straight face as they knowingly reflected on their own experiences with females. Lloyd, meanwhile, was conveying his "now you see what it's like to deal with a human female" look. It was part humor, part exaggerated patience, and part pride in himself for his long-standing relationship with me.

Becoming a bit uncomfortable with their perceptions, I quickly changed the topic off me and onto tattoos. "Could you explain some of the images in the kakau and what they mean," I asked, catching Daisy's eyes looking at me with compassion.

"Absolutely," she said, with the authority of a seasoned speaker, bringing the attention back to herself. "One of our favorite kakau is the mo'o. A lot of Hawaiians, humans that is, think this kakau is a supernatural lizard or a gecko for good health, but it is really a mo'o to which our mo'okane are related. We also use flowers, especially hibiscus and orchid, which are native to Hawaii. Then there is the sea turtle for long life and fertility, and we even have kakau for shells representing wealth and prosperity."

With her last words, the females rose gracefully to their feet in unison. I hastened to do likewise, since it was clear that our time together had come to an end. "Thank you for your explanation," I said to Daisy, "and I hope we will speak again."

"Certainly," she responded smiling, "and tell your leprechaun friend that we enjoyed meeting him as well."

She didn't speak directly to him and, I was intrigued to notice, preferred to send a message through me. Perhaps, that was how it was done in a traditional menehune and mo'okane community with strange males from Ireland. With her last words, she and the others departed almost instantly. Only Lloyd remained.

"All moʻo and menehune, not to mention ancestors, are able to demanifest at will," he said, anticipating my inquiry. "In fact, I think I'll demonstrate right now," he added, laughing at his joke on the human, as he, too, vanished.

Making my way back to Simon, I found him bare-chested dozing in the sun. He stirred when I approached and sat up. "Well, did you meet Leppie?" he asked.

"Yes," I replied, while Simon got up and donned his tee-shirt.

"And what happened?"

"Can I tell you as we walk?" I replied, gazing longingly at the beckoning ocean. "I could use a swim. It would be super if we could just teleport ourselves there as Leppie seems to do, eh."

Later That Afternoon
–The Kahuna Speaks

Later that afternoon, having just returned from a swim in the ocean with Simon, I was sitting alone on the lanai enjoying a glass of chilled white wine, while he enjoyed one of his favorite vacation pastimes inside—surfing the net. Blissfully soaking up the swaying palms, late afternoon sun, and just about everything about this place, I looked at the waves rolling onto the shore in the distance. Questions kept flicking through my mind to ask Lloyd when next he turned up.

"Ask and you shall receive," he greeted me, plopping himself down in a deck chair. He had a fiery burn on all parts of his anatomy that protruded from his bathrobe, and he wore an oversized, wide-brimmed straw hat and whopping sunglasses to shade his beet-red face. The shamrock sarong he wore earlier in the day had left too much of his tender, white flesh exposed. Perhaps to dull the pain, he held a gigantic mai tai in a pint mug.

"You should be careful of those fruit drinks with alcohol," I said, wanting to be helpful, "They pack a much greater wallop than your beloved pint of Guinness."

"You don't need to be worrying about me," he asserted. "If there's one thing I know, it's that I can hold me liquor."

To prove his point, he sucked up a quarter of the mai tai through a fat straw. "That's better," he stated, coming up for air. "What are your questions?"

"First off," I said, taking a large swig of my wine to kid him about holding my liquor, too, "what happened in your ceremony in the mountains yesterday after I left?"

"I was made a kahuna," he smiled proudly.

"That's terrific! Traditionally, aren't there about 40 kinds of kāhuna, such as sorcerers and healers? What kind of kahuna are you?"

"A kahuna can be an expert in many fields, so, OF COURSE, I'm an expert in the field of elementals partnering with humans," he said, lowering his sunglasses and glaring at me over the rim for confirmation.

"That you are," I agreed, "Can you tell me if there are any other kahuna in your field? And does that makes me a kahuna as well?"

"Two questions. Haven't I asked you a million (stressed) times to ask one question at a time? I'll answer the first question first."

"Yes," he stated succinctly, sucking the mai tai.

"A little more information would be appreciated," I said, knowing how much he loved demonstrating his knowledge.

"Since you ask, there are several kāhuna around the world who specialize in elemental and human partnerships, but we only use the term kahuna here in Hawaii. I don't suppose you'd like to know what elementals, like me, need to do to become our version of a kahuna?"

"I'd love to hear," I replied, since he was dying to tell me.

"The first step is to join our order of elementals who want to work with humans, like the menehune and moʻokane of the dunes did today. Second, I find the perfect human for them to partner. By the way, you've been a big help in your workshops and books finding humans who want to partner us elementals."

"Next, the elemental enters into an apprenticeship where us older ones keep them on track with the human to help them stay the course. If they can, they become a medium expert. This continues until they can work with various kinds of humans and elementals. When they finally get that lesson down, they are a real expert. THEN they can go on to the next step. That is to study with other races, like the moʻokane and menehune. We call this advanced study."

Lloyd took a deep breath accompanied by another nip of the mai tai. He was down near the bottom of the mug by now and waiting patiently for me to say something.

"How long does this entire process take?"

"In my case—'cos I'm a fast learner—it took a few decades to learn to work with humans, but some elementals never make it to the finish line. They get kind of bored looking after humans and waiting for them to get the lessons that the elemental is trying to teach," Lloyd exhaled in a what-I-have-to-put-up-with sigh, which I noticed was accompanied by much jiggling of his rotund tummy.

"Thank heavens you've been patient with me and the other humans," I joked, pleased to play his little game. "And how many elementals, like you, go on to advanced study?"

"Oh, that's fairly rare. It's kind of like your Ph.D. It means working with higher frequencies, not the lower ones where most humans exist. You are excluded, me dear, as well as other spiritual humans."

Somewhat mollified, I asked, "So if you're an honorary kahuna, am I one, too?"

"There you go, fishing for a compliment. You fill the kahuna role in this life in many ways. For example, like a kahuna Hawaiians call *kuhikuhi pu'uone* that locate sites to build sacred temples, you took people to sacred sites all over the world for 22 years. Like a *kikokilo*, you predict future events and like a *lapa'au*, you are a healer. You are drawn to Hawaii because you have had many lives here. Even when you dance, your movements are like hula. Still, if you take my advice, it would be best you not go calling yourself a kahuna as it would be sure to ruffle feathers. What you are in the astral world is one thing, and the physical another."

Lloyd sucked up the last drops of his mai tai and got up to go.

"Hold on, you haven't told me about your kahuna initiation ceremony in Kokee yet," I urged.

"You're right," he agreed while departing.

I sat on the lanai and contemplated the leprechaun's words that rang true. I've had flashbacks of living in a traditional Hawaiian village. I was a woman, spending a great deal of time with women and even eating exclusively with them. In those visions I didn't feel constrained by what I intuitively knew was a gender segregation kapu (taboo). Because of these memories, it didn't surprise me that the females on the dunes didn't interact with the males. If one gender spoke, the other refrained. Pondering this further, I was amazed that the male mo'okane on the Wailua River, in Kokee, and on the dunes had conversed with me. I was grateful and deduced that they must know that, if they wish to interact with humans, intergender communication is essential.

Daisy remained an enigma. Not only was she taller and not dressed like the others, but I suspected deep wisdom lay beneath her soft, feminine appearance. Guessing at her reasons for teaching me, I speculated that she was preparing me for something. Much as I loved my leprechaun companion, it was a happy relief to receive a woman friend and supposed this comfort stemmed back to my Hawaiian lives with other women. Was it possible I knew her then?

The days are short in January and dusk was approaching. As I sat musing, a large flock of rose-ringed parakeets descended on the palm trees looking for places to roost for the night. They are amusing and clever and I enjoyed their squawking and acrobatics as they maneuvered into the best places. Originally these birds came from Africa as domestic pets and now they are proliferating in the wild from Holland to Hawaii. In spite of their beauty, they are a scourge to farmers because they eat seeds, fruits, and buds and can devastate orchards in a very short time.

Dark descended and, following the leprechaun's example, I finished off my drink and went inside to make dinner. Fun-filled days with much learning appeared to be the theme of this Hawaiian holiday.

Menehune of the Na Pali Coast

Thirty-eight years ago when I was a young thing, I came to Kauai for the first time with Bill, my partner at the time. Both ardent hikers, especially when nature's beauty called, we asked the locals if there were any good hikes.

"Yes," they said. "One of the best hikes in the world is our Na Pali Coast."

This majestic 6,175-acre state park was only open to foot traffic and the 15 mile- stretch of rugged coastline at the entrance was a Mecca for hikers. They were drawn there by the 4,000-foot cliffs, or *'pali'*, that tower over golden sand beaches and deep jungle valleys.

Within a day, we had loaded our backpacks for a several nights adventure. Unfortunately, we hadn't taken into account the possibility of bad weather. A silly oversight, as our entire experience was dependent on it. The Na Pali Coast is renowned for its high rainfall and we had hiked in rain before... how bad could it be?

The answer is BAD. Rain accompanied us as we started our ascent. Never ones to withdraw from a challenge, we persisted. Up and up we slogged through torrents of running water that had taken the red soil and churned it into slippery mud. We slid off rocks and many times threatened to break an ankle or to fall over the perilous cliffs into the sea below. This went on for about three hours of steep ascent, followed by more hours of steep descent, until we knew defeat and slunk, or should I say, slid our way back to the start of the path. Absolutely sodden and disappointed, we thanked the gods and goddesses of the mountain that we were still intact.

So here we are in present day. I am with a new partner, one who has had a triple bypass. And I have been out of commission for a year with a back injury from a car accident. But… it's a beautiful day and we find ourselves at 3:40 p.m. at Keʻe Beach, which is the start of the Na Pali Coast trail.

"Let's do the first leg of the trail," I suggested to Simon. "After all, it's only four miles long and we can easily be back before dark." Evidently I have a short memory.

Simon agreed and we prepared to leave. We each had a half bottle of water, but how much could we need? He was going to wear sandals, but remembering the rocks on this trail, I urged him to put on running shoes.

And we're off! Starting in good cheer, we were puffing and sweating within minutes. Descending the same path we were struggling to ascend, we met other hikers on their return. Despite their walking sticks and poles, their legs were covered in mud and some blood and, since I'd left my hiking pole at home, I regarded theirs with envy.

Up and up we climbed and, when the scenery became ever more beautiful, our commitment to our adventure deepened. In the back of my mind was the ever-present hope that perhaps the menehune of the Na Pali Coast would come speak with me. After all, I was loyally following the instructions of the rainbow deva at the secret falls.

After an hour we reached the summit and saw the towering cliffs ahead and the blue sea breaking waves beneath us. Gorgeous, and better still, no rain. We started our descent into what we thought was the next valley and our final destination, only to have the path at the bottom begin to ascend again. Not to be discouraged, we continued through streams crossing our path and past tinkling, magical waterfalls. Lush green ferns, diverse palms, wild ginger, and an abundance of yellow, blue, and white wildflowers fed my sight, while friendly birds, singing and calling to each other, accompanied us. Especially noticeable were brilliant, red cardinals and cute, rust-breasted finches with grey and white-tipped wings that fluttered about keeping us company.

Up and down we tromped, taking many stops for breath and frugal sips of water. Drenched with sweat, we finally commenced the final descent into the Hanakapi'ai Valley where we'd heard there was a sandy beach. I don't know where the beach was supposed to be because ten-foot waves crashing against black, volcanic boulders greeted us. Carefully climbing to get closer, but not too close, to the shore, we encountered a series of signs warning us to stay away from the treacherous beach. Even when calm, the rip currents can easily drag you out to sea and one sign said that 86 unfortunates were known to have lost their lives at that location.

Because we were the last ones to begin the trail, it was late in the day by the time we reached the beach. There, amidst the immense boulders, and surrounded by dense forest and wild guava plants, we stood in awe of the towering waves. Behind us, in what was by now a dark valley, we could hear a crashing waterfall. Simon, always the daredevil, climbed along the slippery rocks to feel the power of the sea and to record his exploit on camera with a selfie. I clung to safer ground hoping that number 87 wouldn't be lost that day.

Amidst these powerful, breathtaking forces of nature, I felt menehune watching me.

"Welcome sister, we greet you," a mocha-skinned, slender menehune, carrying a long, wooden walking pole, walked into view, followed by more smiling menehune who resembled forest elves.

"We have been awaiting your arrival."

His warmth was a pleasant surprise, given that it's usually Lloyd who receives the accolades with me along as the sidekick. Not that I'd have it any other way. I'm happy that he has included me on so many expeditions to meet elementals and other races.

Reading my mind, the menehune continued, "We're always pleased to see Lloyd, but it's you we want to speak with today. We're the menehune of the northern shore and now you've met the menehune of all four directions. Our ancestors wanted nothing to do with the haole, white humans like you, when they first arrived, so we came to this remote area. In fact, not many of us wanted anything to do with humans. Period. However, a handful of us have joined Lloyd's group to learn how to co-create with humans. We know it's necessary to do this to save menehune and the Earth.

"We preserve the old Hawaiian culture, and there have been a few humans who respected our traditions that have lived in isolated valleys along this coast. A small number still do and go only once or twice a year to Lihue, or Hanalei, to get supplies they cannot find here. We're not a social community; we like to be alone. Our north shore is inaccessible, so humans have not encroached on us.

Because of this, our members have not dwindled as much as the menehune in other parts of Kauai."

I listened in silence absorbing what he wished to share. When he had finished speaking, I asked, "Is there anything you would have me know about your north shore community and how it differs from the others?"

"Only what we're speaking of," he replied succinctly.

"Do you use any skills that differ from the other menehune?" I probed.

"We've hunted whales in the past, but we don't do it much now. We communicate with the whales, sharks, and great sea beings and Kanaloa, the god of the ocean, is our deity and great friend."

Curious about a mysterious group of menehune said to have once lived on the Na Pali Coast, I asked, "Could you tell me something of the 'lost tribe' who lived in the Honopu Valley along this coast until the mid-nineteenth century? I've heard that archaeologists found skulls of primitive pre-Hawaiian people living in that valley."

"The skulls are those of hybrids, resulting from the mating of menehune and humans," he answered. "Menehune interbred with Polynesian humans in the early days, because our two peoples had much in common, such as respect for the land and all growing things. Humans living in remote valleys along the coast respected and knew our people, so this was a natural process, and both of our races benefited from this contact."

"I heard that, when Europeans and Americans did a census, 80 Hawaiian families said they had menehune blood."

"This is true, but humans, especially haole, don't always believe what they're told." His smile contained the slightest hint of sarcasm.

If there was ever a believer in hybrids, it was me, so it was easy to reply, "I do believe your story, and this would mean that menehune are physical ancestors of many humans living in Hawaii today."

"Yes, but we're more than that. Humans, especially western scientists, believe that hybrids can only be created by physically fertilizing one being with the genetic material from another kind of being. However, the spiritual essence of two beings is also passed to their hybrids. I see you understand this, but there is something important that you don't recognize. You, like so many haole, have a blind spot."

"Please tell me what I don't see and hopefully I will be able to change it in the future," I implored.

"That is the problem exactly," he countered with frustration. "Although you are able to speak with beings like us who live in different dimensions, which is a true understanding of spacial existence, you are not nearly as good at comprehending time. You see time as linear, from past to present to future. Hawaiians, like other Indigenous peoples, know this isn't the case. All exists now. Your next step will be to realize that your ancestors are alive and affecting you, both physically, and spiritually this very day. Unfortunately, haole have lost this connection with the ancestors and we, along with ancestors in other countries, are attempting to renew this broken link. The first step is for people to believe in us. How else would we be able to help you?"

I knew in theory he was correct and that all exists in the present. Haven't all spiritual teachers said this? Still there was a gap between the theory and living this practice for me. While I pondered the task, the menehune gave me another one.

"Also," he said, "you may want to consider who are your Hawaiian ancestors?" With this quixotic message, he withdrew his energy, signaling that our talk was over.

I realized this was the first time that I'd seen menehune without moʻokane. And the difference between them was becoming increasingly blurred for me, because many of them were of similar size, body shape, and coloring. Not to mention they wore the same type of clothes. Is it possible that they were also interbreeding to form hybrids?

Daylight was fading quickly, and I returned my attention to our trek. At that moment, I saw Simon wave victoriously from the top of a steep rock. It was cooler now, and inspired by the menehune, I pondered his message as we started walking.

Although we were careful with our footing, several times we slipped in the mud and almost fell on the sharp rocks. We lapsed into silence and gradually, as evening advanced, we descended once again to the start of the trail minutes before total darkness. Tired and full…a lovely day.

Elementals of Maui

The raucous parakeet flocks awakened me before sunrise. Pulling myself into a chair on the lanai, I wrapped myself in a blanket to hold off the morning chill, and was sitting there quietly when my leprechaun friend arrived. He was wrapped in a blanket, too, one that bore a remarkable resemblance to mine.

"Your hiking yesterday was really impressive. Well done, for an old gal like you," he laughed, the only one on the lanai to find his words amusing.

"I couldn't fail to notice your absence on the hike," I responded, "Too strenuous for you?"

"Never. We Irish are fitter than North Americans."

The words "like you" remained unspoken, but implied.

I changed the topic to my unanswered questions. "Joking aside, I'm interested in knowing more about the moʻokane and their relationship with the menehune. Also, are there any elementals in Hawaii?"

"Let's start with elementals (his favorite topic, given that he is one). When you were in Maui a few years back, you had two experiences with elementals," he replied.

Momentarily confused by his comment, I recalled the time when I was in the sacred Iao Valley in Maui hiking with some friends. The main attraction of the valley is the Iao Needle, which is an extension of the cliffs of the West Maui Mountains, and the site of an extinct volcano. Busloads of tourists were gathered at the entrance to look at the Needle, but my friends and I were more interested in the deserted valley. In ancient times, the valley was kapu (taboo) to all but Hawaiian royalty who both lived and buried their dead here. Hawaiian ali'i believed that the *mana*, the spiritual life force of their bones, could give power to their enemies, even harm their descendants, so they kept this sacred burial area off limits.

The power of the valley is palpable, which is probably why the ali'i originally chose to live here, and also why Maui's army selected this location to fight King Kamehameha the Great when he invaded in 1790. Kamehameha defeated the Maui warriors and, with their mana and that of the ancestors buried in the valley, he was able to unite all of Hawaii under his rule.

We wandered peacefully beside the river and were winding our way back, when I felt called by unseen beings to gather my friends along the bank.

Sensing a presence behind me, I turned around to see a beautiful, mist-covered mountain peak from which a large, light being descended into the valley to speak with us. Like the deva of the secret falls at Uluwehi, this being was female. Her body was indistinct except for her triangular-shaped face, slightly-slanted eyes, and a spiked corona around her head that resembled hair standing straight up. She shimmered with light.

"Welcome to my sacred valley. I am the guardian who resides here," she addressed me. "I hear in your thoughts that your first impression relates me to the ones called the children of the mist by the first peoples of New Zealand."

"Those beings are related to the Sidhe of Ireland," I acknowledged, telepathically. "Is that true of you as well?"

"I don't see myself as limited by your definition, but there is a relationship. Have you noticed that all of us live in the mist? These misty places were chosen by the Hawaiian aliʻi because we, the protectors of the land, are here. The veil between the physical world and the higher realms of the gods is thin in this valley. Because of this, the aliʻi and certain priestly branches of the kāhuna could align themselves to the sacred divine ways of Spirit and communicate with us more easily here. We are the teachers, the guardians, the ancestors. We are the mouthpiece of the gods."

Awed by her pure presence, I eagerly shared her message with my friends. Wanting to gift her, we used the river waters in that sacred valley to purify and open our hearts to more deeply love her and the feminine heart of Maui. When finished, my friends walked on ahead. That's when I became aware of small beings walking towards me. They were greenish, about waist height, and had long arms and legs. They had red hair that stood on end like the corona of the deva of the mist.

The deva noticed that my attention had been diverted to the smaller beings and said, "I am an ancestor of these little ones. They are related to the race you think of as elementals."

One of the smaller, human-like beings spoke to me. "We've lived in this valley since ancient times and we taught the first Hawaiians how to live in harmony with the land according to nature's plan. The streams of four rivers flow through this plain. Therefore, more crops were grown here than in the rest of Maui, and thousands of humans lived in the vicinity.

We helped the men to grow over 300 varieties of taro in the valley and to prepare it as food. We taught the Hawaiians that taro is an elder brother and, even today, taro is sacred and no one is allowed to fight or argue in front of a bowl of poi, which is made from the taro. Taro isn't only a starch food, you know. It has heart-shaped leaves and, as its body resembles that of a human, we treat it also as a medicine."

When the small greenish being finished speaking, he looked to my right side and, following his gaze, I saw Lloyd listening to the explanation. Having no memory of him being there when this experience occurred, I was surprised to see him.

"That's because I wasn't here THEN," he said smiling. "Have you forgotten that elementals can travel, not only in space, but also in time? I wanted to accompany you to this time to help you remember that you'd met these elementals in Maui a few years ago. You didn't ask them what race they belonged to, so they didn't tell you."

When Lloyd was speaking, the scarlet-haired elemental listened respectfully. After the leprechaun had finished, he spoke to me, "I'm happy Lloyd brought you to meet us again. Your memories of the various mo'okane and menehune you've met on Kauai are recorded in your mana, your life force energy, which you refer to both as your etheric blueprint and your body elemental. We guardians of nature read this blueprint, as easily as you think and speak. Therefore, we're able to share the experiences that you've had with our brothers and sisters on Kauai.

I was fascinated by how these beings were able to meet others through my memories of them. "Why don't you go to visit them when it's that easy for you to travel in space and time?"

"True, it is easy," the small being stated. "However, we like to hear your thoughts about them, because when we're in your physical presence, your mana changes us."

"For the good, I take it?" I inquired smiling.

"Absolutely!"

During our conversation, my friend remained silent. He now decided to improve my faulty memory once more. "You've travelled in space and time, just like elementals. Remember the first time you went to Egypt! You were staying in a hotel near the Great Pyramid and at midnight you heeded an internal call to go to the pyramids. Then what happened?"

"I was walking towards the pyramids in the darkness when, all of a sudden, I found myself in another physical body, and in bright daylight walking along the same path. I'll never forget this experience, as it totally confirmed for me the theory that there is no such thing as space and time. It was as real as the physical world. There was no difference. In less than a second, I saw individuals lining the path playing ancient instruments. I 'knew' everything about life in Egypt in those days, and about the life of the woman I was then, including her name and what she did. Is that the way it is for you elementals when you travel in space and time?"

"It's identical," replied the leprechaun. "All humans will do this in their near future, when they'll be conscious in the etheric and astral realms where elementals, menehune, and moʻokane exist. At that time, they'll be able to see and communicate with us, and other great beings, like the deva of this valley."

"My heavens!" I said to Lloyd. "Yesterday the menehune on the Na Pali Coast said I needed to become aware of how all time exists in the present. I only just remembered this now and you triggered this memory by having me recall my Egyptian experiences. Was this intentional on your part?"

"Of course. What happened to you yesterday is present for me today, even as the menehune told you. I wanted you to recall that you have already experienced this reality."

At that moment the elemental interrupted to say goodbye, "It was nice meeting you, however we need to get back to work tending the growing beings in the valley. Now that humans are no longer growing taro here, we have other plants to look after. Plus, some of us travel daily to the fields where we help humans to grow taro."

My conversations with the deva, elemental, and Lloyd took place in instantaneous time. This is the way it happens with telepathy. The complete sights, words, and experience impress me at once. It's instantaneous and recorded in the ethers that I can attune to at any time. The menehune's comments had brought what is instinctive to me into conscious awareness.

Lloyd accompanied me back to the car. "I did say that you had two experiences with elementals in Maui. That was the first one; do you recall the second?"

It was only a week after the first experience. At that time, four friends and I were visiting the Kula Botanical Garden near Keokea. The garden was stunning, full of native Hawaiian plants and, as I wandered through, I saw an elemental being watching me. He was similar to the ones I'd met in the Iao Valley, but taller, chest height, with spiked red hair that resembled the corona of the deva there. Wearing an apron, carrying a shovel, he approached me to speak.

"My hair is spiked so I can receive energy, 'mana' we say, directly from the sun for nourishment," he volunteered, anticipating my inquiry. "The beings you met in the Iao Valley and I are able to take the energy we receive from the sun and give it directly to plants to help them grow. Although there is a human who claims that title, I'm the head gardener here. I work directly with him, guiding him. I like working in this garden because many plants are native to Maui. My fellow gardeners and I have no wish to go anywhere else."

As the gardener spoke, he looked further along the path to where similar beings were digging in the soil. Like him, they wore aprons and giggled shyly when I looked at them.

"We weed out the plants that are too abundant and fertilize the others with the organic matter that is produced in decay," the head gardener said. "We do this by asking the elements of water and air to give each plant what it needs. Humans can do this, too, if they only use their minds and thoughts to ask for it."

Always eager to be a better gardener, I inquired, "How else do you help the plants to grow?"

"By giving them energy and appreciation. All beings thrive on love."

His words immediately cast me back into my own garden. I saw myself wandering through the garden admiring and talking to the flowers, bushes, and trees. I'd compliment some on how well they were doing. For those who looked sickly, I'd ask what they needed (more water or less shade) and then attempt to provide it for them.

Reading my thoughts, the head gardener said, "That's it exactly. That's how you feed each plant."

Bringing my thoughts back to his garden, I asked, "Where is the best place to go in your garden?"

"Why, wherever you are is always the best," he said, laughing. "I must return to my work now. Enjoy."

Lloyd was observing me. "The gardeners here, and the little one in the Iao Valley, are appearing to you only in one of the forms that they could choose. Mo'o, elementals, and ancestral spirits, are able to choose many forms, depending on the element in which they are strong, their individual strength, and their original ancestry."

"Why is it that I always see you looking the same then?" I inquired.

"This is the form that you and I both prefer, so why not?" he laughed and vanished.

I had a feeling that more information would be forthcoming in either his, or Spirit's, timing. It turned out that this would take much longer than I'd expected. The leprechaun was absent for the remainder of my time in Kauai and neither the menehune, nor mo'okane seemed interested in sharing more with me. In other words, I got the vacation I thought I wanted.

A Year Later: The Dunes Again

During the following months, back in Canada, the many experiences in Kauai were becoming rooted in me. But the process was not complete. The more I reached to understand the moʻokane, menehune, and ancestors, the more they eluded me. Yet, conversely I felt them orchestrating my journey, teasing me along, and arranging opportunities for contacting me. I yearned for the soft, spiritual, yin energy of Kauai and, as synchronicity would have it, three organizations on the Hawaiian Islands invited me to speak at their events.

I rented a condo sight unseen and on arrival discovered that our unit overlooked Prince Kuhio Park where an ancient heiau (temple) was located. While Simon opted for a nap, I went directly to the park to see if any ancestors would speak with me. Entering the park, I noticed that I was the only visitor, which was strange, given the importance of this historical site and its central location. Respectfully, I walked closer to the heiau and sat at the entrance without touching the stones.

Immediately, two tall warrior human ancestors appeared wearing golden and red feather cloaks with matching feather helmets on their heads. They held spears at their sides in a non-threatening stance. While the warriors didn't speak, I felt their task was to prohibit humans from going inside the heiau, or touching the stones, because this would remove energy from the site.

Even though the heiau was no longer complete in the physical realm, it was whole in the etheric and astral realms. The ancestors didn't want that heiau, or any sacred site, contaminated by new age people with conflicting philosophies. Even if these warriors had nothing against me personally, they didn't want to dilute their energy, the energy of the heiau, or the work they did.

Puzzled about what to do, as Spirit and the ancestors obviously had brought me to this location, I sent a telepathic call to Lloyd and he arrived without delay.

"Lloyd, will they speak with you?" I inquired.

"No," he replied, "They don't wish to speak to me either."

"Do you have any idea what they're trying to convey to us with their silent presence?"

"Yes...that we, and they, only need to be. As far as they are concerned, speaking is not necessary to communicate what they want. It was kapu for the royal ali'i, like these ones, to speak with commoners and strangers. It confuses them that, although you are a haole because you are a non-native Hawaiian, you have a lot of power, a lot of mana, which is usually the realm only of kāhuna (shaman) and royalty. Therefore, they're not sure what to do with you."

"Why don't they speak with you?"

"I'm a foreigner as well," he responded, nudging me in the ribs.

"I have a feeling these ancestors wait for something to fall into place—perhaps concerning us. Do you have the same feeling?" I nudged him back.

"Absolutely. Best to stay in the present moment of being, as moving into the future takes away your mana," he smiled, always pleased with himself to be giving advice to the human.

"I read about Prince Kuhio on that plaque," I said, pointing to the sign at the entrance. "Prince Kuhio descended from the kings and queens of Hawaii and he headed the Royal Order of Kamehameha I whose mission was to perpetuate Hawaiian culture. In fact, the Hawaiian Islands still celebrate him and this location is his birthplace."

"And guess who is an honorary member of a branch of this order?" Lloyd beamed, sticking his chest out.

"Don't tell me. You?"

"You got it! It's only for us men. However, there's a woman's sub-branch," he, emphasized the word "sub", just spoiling for an argument.

"Speaking of sub-branches, which sub-branch do you belong to?" I smiled, also emphasizing "sub".

"The branch for the various kinds of elementals and menehune, of course. I've been taking my study of Hawaiian culture seriously now that I'm an honorary kahuna and all."

"What particular area are you studying?" I requested, hoping to receive answers from my elusive companion.

"That's a BIG surprise I've got planned, but it's not quite ready. More rehearsals are needed."

With those puzzling words, my leprechaun friend bowed respectfully to the guardian ancestors and vanished. Following his example, I thanked them as well and, remaining in a non-attached state, slowly walked back to my condo. Because I intended to sleep outside overlooking this sacred place, I had a strong intuition that the Hawaiian ancestors would influence me then. So why not enjoy the rest of the day!

Given that several hours of daylight still remained, Simon and I decided to enjoy a walk on the dunes. Simon, always keen to try something new, studied a tourist brochure and discovered the Makauwahi Cave, located further north than the dunes we had explored the previous year. I whole-heartedly agreed, so we hopped in the car and set off. A bit vague on directions, we found ourselves driving on a dusty track lacking signposts and were starting to doubt ourselves when we came across a lone car and a man getting out of it.

"Hi," Simon said, leaning out the window, "Are we going the right way for a large cave?"

"Makauwahi. Absolutely!" the man answered smiling. "I'm Richard Segan, a volunteer guide, and I'm on my way there right now."

Luck was with us. Falling in behind Richard, we followed him down a narrow winding path and soon found ourselves overlooking Makauwahi, the largest cave in the Hawaiian Islands and the only one not created by a volcano.

Richard, a volunteer for the preservation of the cave, gave us an introduction to the site and showed us bones of extinct birds found there. Although the archeological information was interesting, I was keener to learn about the spiritual practices of the Hawaiians in this cave. According to Richard, an elder interviewed in the1880s spoke about a seer who had lived in the cave. The seer sat on a platform (Richard pointed it out), and answered questions from Hawaiians who sought him for advice. The questioners threw special leaves onto the seer's fire; the seer then read the smoke to answer the questions. In fact, the cave's name, Makauwahi, actually means "smoke eye".

Leaving Richard and Simon and moving deeper into the cave, faces of seers, whose energies still protected this place, bombarded me. The ancestors at heiaus would not speak to me, so I was caught by surprise when these ancestors did.

"Both the heiaus and this cave have spiritual importance for us," I heard. "But here we follow the traditions of kāhuna, not the ali'i, so it's not kapu for us to speak with you. We wish to give you information to share with others, so they will respect the spiritual sacredness as well as the archeological importance of this place.

"We seers performed ceremonies and initiations here and the last seer knew us and respected our traditions. For many generations, kāhuna and ali'i contacted Mother Earth by coming to this cave. They came when they entered puberty or, if they had an important quest to do for the people, such as going on a sea voyage. When we buried important people here, the men stood on one side of the cave and the women on the other. Otherwise, men and woman came separately to speak with us and we used herbs to create different kinds of smoke depending on their question."

Looking more deeply, I witnessed that Hawaiians also came to the cave for protection, if their homes were invaded. But mostly they came to be in contact with Mother Earth and for deep seeing in their visions. I thanked the ancestral seers for speaking with me and, returning to Richard, shared what I'd been told. Richard confirmed what the ancestors said and elaborated, "Yes, both the seer's father and grandfather were seers in this cave."

At that moment more people arrived for Richard to help. So we left and continued walking along the coast. Being more scientific, the archeology intrigued Simon, but what the ancestors said to me also interested him. I had just finished telling him their message when I heard voices from unseen beings asking me to take a barely discernible path deeper into the forest. While I followed the call through the trees, Simon sat down on the cliff, content to watch the mating humpback whales cavorting in the distance.

The stern mo'okane, whom I'd met in the dunes a year earlier, soon manifested before me on the path. Deeply tanned with a shell lei circling his neck, he wore a grass loincloth and stood holding a spear.

"Aloha, sister. We are happy to see you again. Come rest beside our tree."

With those words, the mo'okane pointed to a large tree where I could sit out of the sun. Astonished to be called "sister", my heart flew open with his words. I felt welcomed in a way that I hadn't in our previous meeting.

"We tend to be people who seek the shade," he said, bypassing my emotional reaction to his greeting. "We emerge early in the morning before the sun rises and then again at dusk and into the night. Because of our mo'o heritage, we seek the mist, water, and rain. We love the rain to fall on our skin, go down our throats, cleanse, purify, and invigorate us. In the sun we feel slow, sluggish and, even though we live in these hot dunes, there are cool places like this one. Here a breeze always blows. Plus, if we are too hot, we can always go for a swim."

"I'm a bit confused," I ventured. "Because you are related to lizards and dragons, I'd think that you'd love the sun."

"We enjoy some heat, especially those of our tribe who live in the dunes. But all moʻo are devoted to the element of water, just as our sister Pele on the Big Island is devoted to the element of fire. Even most of our food comes from the water. We eat fish and, because we sing their song, they come to our spears and give us their lives."

He smiled as he spoke, revealing his razor-sharp teeth.

"My teeth seem to bother you," he said, frowning, and his moʻo dragon-like facial tattoos took on a menacing appearance. "You have drifted far from your roots. We don't find this appealing."

Shamed by his comments, I replied, "I apologize, but meeting moʻokane has been unnerving in some ways." I shared the image of how severe he'd been the last time we met. "Also, I'm uncertain as to what you want from me, and Lloyd has been little help."

His tattoos took on a friendlier appearance. "We are reawakening your ancestral memories and your connection with us."

"It would help if you shared your name, so I don't think of you as the moʻokane with the frightening tattoos."

Flashing his glistening teeth, his moʻo tattoos accompanied him in laughter. "Call me Burt," he answered.

Burt suddenly vanished and Daisy, whom I'd met in the dunes the previous year, appeared. She wore a wreath in her long dark hair and her gently rounded body was robed in a blue and white flowered muumuu. Her gold-flecked black eyes sparkled with intelligent warmth, underlaid with a sense of mischief. Burt had disappeared, I surmised, because in traditional Hawaiian culture males and females do not associate with each other. But then, why did he speak with me?

"On these islands the beliefs of those who keep to the traditional ways, whether they are menehune, moʻokane, or human ancestors are the same," Daisy volunteered, acknowledging my thoughts. "Burt (she said smiling) exempts you from our kapu, our taboos, since you are both a haole and modern human.

"Moʻokane, like Burt, are related to moʻo, although they're choosing a human form. Menehune, moʻo, and human ancestors in the astral realms are all guardians of the Earth. We travel back and forth to each other's realms to work together and with elementals like your leprechaun friend. All of us are ancestors, however it's essential you do not think of us in the past tense, because we ancestors are alive and influencing you and others in the present."

What a relief to have someone help me understand more about the relationship between all kinds of ancestors. Perhaps Daisy would answer other questions that Lloyd seemed unwilling, or unable, to answer.

"I know that menehune and humans interbred to create hybrids who look like regular humans, but who carry this distinct lineage," I said. "But sometimes I'm having difficulty telling the differences between moʻokane and menehune. Did they interbreed to create hybrids, too?"

"The short answer is 'Yes'", she laughed gently at what I could only guess was my haole way of wanting to simplify everything.

"And the long answer?"

"In the astral world, everyone can create any body they want and beings of different races who work closely together tend to take on characteristics of the other. The moʻo taught the menehune who, in turn, taught the original Polynesians who came to Hawaii. In this way, the moʻo are the ancestors of both menehune and humans. The moʻokane, are a version of moʻo, who chose a human form to relate more easily both to menehune and humans."

My eyeballs must have been rolling. Daisy chose an example closer to home. "Think of it this way. Your leprechaun friend can choose any form, yet he prefers to have a human-like one because he works with humans. And as he works with humans, he becomes more like them. Same with you. As you work with him and us, you become more like us. Our spiritual essence mingles together and you become more of a hybrid. This has happened in many of your lives and it's being reactivated in this life."

Don't we all love hearing about ourselves, so I was ready to go into my lives with menehune and moʻo, however Daisy had a different plan.

"We've noticed that sometimes it's difficult for you to tell the difference between menehune and human ancestors, so I've come to help," she said, changing the topic to what she obviously wanted to discuss. "We have many classes and kinds of menehune and, unlike the slender elves you know from Ireland, menehune are Polynesian so they look more like human Polynesians. It may be confusing as the menehune of both the royal aliʻi and kāhuna shaman are physically larger and taller than the little child-size ones that humans most commonly encounter who they refer to as the menehune."

"So how do I tell the difference?" I asked, totally confused by her explanation.

"It's not important that you do," replied Daisy, leaning forward. "The teachings are the teachings whether they come from the moʻo, the moʻokane, the menehune, or human kāhuna. You haoles seek to categorize and divide. We Hawaiians seek wholeness—to bring everything together into unity. We seek an effortless flow with no barriers or hard places between our learnings, teachings, ways of life—all in harmony with the Earth."

She then changed her topic entirely and ventured into an area she obviously felt I could better grasp. "I know you are frustrated that your leprechaun friend is not around much to help you understand what we are teaching you. But he can't help you because he is only a student himself and must not speak about what he does not know. Lloyd spends a lot of time with our elders, our *kupuna*. We teach him our ways. You would call them 'yin' teachings. We think of them as 'being' teachings. Being for us means aligning yourself to Spirit, going with the flow, paddling in the direction that Spirit wants to lead you, and not forcing your will on others. It involves listening deeply to your conscience and doing what it tells you. It means listening to the inner guides, the ancestors who are trying to help you. In doing this, you gain peace, harmony, and serve your purpose in the physical life you have presently.

"Lloyd is in the stage of life where he needs to be trained in how to be. Being is more of a feminine quality and, because he is over-developed in his masculine 'yang' side, he needs to learn being. After a while, being and doing merge. When this happens the individual has earned the term elder—kupuna. Lloyd cannot study being from you, because humans, especially you haole, are more doers than be-ers. In early life, humans master how to do, but in middle age they should master how to be, to ripen like a fruit. This is not a chastisement; it is a fact."

"I recognize the importance of what you are saying, not only for Lloyd, but for me and all humans," I acknowledged. "Being is a quality I value highly; yet, I find it easier to take action to attain my goals."

"If you sit in your center and visualize what you wish," Daisy said, her black eyes sending me a powerful image, "you attract everything to you. If you go racing after what you think you want, you often drive it away. For many haole, the amount of energy they use craving something equals the energy of fear and doubt that they won't get it. If you sit in your center, on the other hand, you have no fear or doubt. You dream the dream and it comes to you. You call this meditation and this is how we ancestors manifest."

Changing her direction yet again, Daisy stood up and dusted the sand from her muumuu, "That's enough for today. Our way of teaching is to give you the right amount of food to digest, so you don't overeat. By the way, there is a quiet beach further north along the dunes where you could have a swim to cool off."

After she left, I sat for a short time reflecting on her visit. I was intrigued that a kahuna was taking the time to teach me and wondered if I'd become Daisy's project. That was a nice idea, as I was honored by her time and felt a relationship building between us. I still couldn't figure out if Daisy were a menehune or human ancestor, but knew to leave that question in abeyance as she had requested. Not easy, given my western brain, but I surrendered to trust the process.

Emerging from the forest, I saw that Simon had his binoculars trained on the whales. Putting them down, he asked, "Did they talk to you?"

I was as happy to share, as he was to hear. It was sweltering in the full heat of the day and, eager to find the beach Daisy had mentioned, we headed north along the path. About half an hour later, after walking past breathtaking views, we arrived at a sheltered cove where pristine water kissed the shore. Some two-dozen people had also discovered the cove and were making a day of it, lying on their blankets and drinking beer. I could hardly wait to go in. Only one problem: no bathing suit.

Pondering my dilemma, I looked around for privacy only to find Himself in the shade of an old tree lounging in a hammock. He wore oversized sunglasses with a large sombrero and beside him on a table rested a gigantic mug with "mai tai" written on it. His swimming costume looked like it had come from a 1920s catalogue. It was one piece from shoulders to knees in his favorite green color. Lifting his sombrero, and eyeing me over the top of his sunglasses, he gestured me over.

"A problem with no swim suit, me dear?" he smiled, all-knowingly. "The water is lovely, by the way."

"I thought you were so busy studying with the elders that you had no time for playing."

"It's afternoon break. They don't work in Hawaii near the amount we do in Ireland. I've been struggling to convert, as you can see?"

"My new kahuna friend said you were studying 'being'. I'm ready to study some of that myself!"

"Then you'd best get your clothes off and into the water, don't you think?" he prodded, knowing I was shy about swimming in public in my underwear.

Taking up the challenge, I stripped off my outer clothes and, free like a child, cast myself into the welcoming ocean. Looking back to see my friend, I saw that he had left. Gone back to work, I imagined, while I floated on my back and let the ocean carry me where it would.

Encounter with Ancient Ocean Mo'o

I met Danny at a conference in Lihue where I spoke about hybrids. He was intrigued when I said some humans had dragon ancestors and that these dragons were related to the mo'o of Hawaii. Wanting to share what he knew, Danny invited Simon and I to meet the ancient mo'o of Kalihiwai Point, called by local's the Dragon's Breath, on the northern coast of Kauai.

The Dragon's Breath is a sacred site to Kauaians and I felt honored that a local like Danny wished to take us. Unfortunately, the water dragon lives in a difficult to reach sea cave at the base of a cliff. Preparing to descend the cliff, I put on my hiking boots and observed Danny removing his sandals to hike barefoot.

"I've been hiking barefoot since I was a kid," Danny explained, "and I can grip the earth better in my bare feet."

Not attempting to imitate his example, I laced my boots tighter and pushed through the clumps of thorny bougainvillea. Danny led us quickly along the path and I was doing fine until we reached a fifty-foot drop. Grasping a rope, Danny threw himself backwards down the cliff expecting me to follow. After much positive self-talk and encouragement from the stronger-armed men, I seized the rope and took a step. Committed now, I slid down the cliff backwards holding the rope for dear life. Arriving at the bottom safely, I turned around amidst large, volcanic rocks to face a roaring sea. The waves surged in with immense force hitting the back of the sea cave that Hawaiians believe represents the dragon's mouth. The waves then bounced back and spit the water through the mouth and nostril of the dragon to create what Danny described as a fine mist.

Speaking loudly over the roar of the waves, Danny came closer and said, "In the Hawaiian tradition, sharing breath is very important and here we're sharing breath with the mo'o."

At that moment a rogue wave rushed in and drenched us. So much for the "fine mist". I left Simon and Danny to discuss waves and currents and quickly set out for a dryer area towards the dragon's tail, where I hoped to speak with the mo'o. Trying to avoid one unpleasantness, I instantly encountered another by falling into a crevice and gashing my leg on the sharp, volcanic stone. This may seem strange, but somehow it felt appropriate after being purified by water to make a blood offering to the mo'o.

Carefully now, lest a more serious offering be demanded, I continued on my way and came to a large channel cut into the rock. Overlooking the channel was a craggy boulder that resembled the dragon-like face of a large mo'o standing guard. Knowing this was the place to stop, I gingerly perched on a rock and waited. Sensing myself assessed by a powerful presence, I remained immobile, as a massive, water dragon slowly swam up the channel. The mo'o's skin was smooth unlike the scales that are often associated with land-dwelling dragons.

No introductions were forthcoming as it examined me with cool ancient eyes. "I greet you in this form, because I prefer this dragon shape, after all it is our original form."

Amazed at its size and not a little intimidated by the power, the mana, I felt streaming from it, I struggled to say something meaningful and came up with "How large are you?"

"I am as long as I am. We do not measure as humans do. We continue to grow as we age, and I'm the largest and oldest mo'o amidst the Hawaiian Islands. My strength comes from the ocean. However, I guard the caves and waterfalls of this shore, too.

"Until now, I've only met mo'o that resemble mist, or have taken human-like forms. Could you tell me how ocean mo'o differ?"

"We think of ourselves as ancestors, or lesser gods. We ocean mo'o don't think of ourselves as mo'okane, who have chosen a human form to live on land. Mo'okane have diverged from our path in evolution and are a sub-race to ours. We are more closely related to the mo'o who protect the ponds and springs. We, of the saltwater, have the most power because the others have abandoned their strength to become land dwellers.

"We meet together to discuss how to keep the ocean clean, and how to work with the currents, fish, and water dwellers in order to create balance. Our work with humans varies. In the old days, we were close to fishermen and those who travelled the ocean in large canoes. Humans, who knew the ocean, prayed in temples dedicated to us. Now this has changed because boats are mechanized, and we have no affinity with mechanization.

"Even now, some of us elect to work with humans. One of these is Kimokeo Kapahulehua, who is working to preserve water on the islands. He looks after the fish and taro ponds that are sacred to us. He has also been taking men on *wa'a* (canoe) voyages to link the ancestral routes through the Hawaiian Islands. He honors our gift of bringing humans to Hawaii and establishes a link for us to guide humans on their future paths."

Meeting Kimokeo some years earlier in Maui occurred in a very roundabout way. One of my German students who came to Maui for her graduation from our institute met him canoeing and introduced us.

"You are a kupuna," Kimokeo said to me. "Kupuna are elders with knowledge and experience that makes them wise. They give this to their *'ohana* (family, kin group). When we speak of a kupuna of the natural elements, we are speaking of the people of the heavens, Na Poe La Lani; the ocean, Na Poe Ka Moana; and the land, Na Poe Ka Honua. The Na Poe Ka Lani, the elders of the Heaven, are all the natural elements, such as stars, moon, sun, clouds, winds, and power, such as waves, tides, currents, hurricanes, and storms. The Na Poe Ka Moana are all the fish, corals, seaweed, octopuses, whales, dolphins, and sharks. The Na Poe Ka Honua are the people of the earth or land ('aina), such as humans, trees, birds, insects, all animals, and birds.

"When I think of you and call you a kupuna, it is the spiritual being, not necessarily the physical being…like the whale. The whale is the physical mammal of the ocean, but he is also the elder, a kupuna of the ocean, with power to navigate from one place to another through the natural elements. As a Ke alakai kou mau kupuna, you are the pathway of our ancestors."

I felt a kinship with Kimokeo, although outwardly I had little in common with a Hawaiian man who took people on canoe voyages. Each time I saw or spoke with him, this feeling of kinship deepened and awakened in me a desire to more fully understand his chosen paths. At that time I had never heard of the moʻo, so I felt there might be a kinship between Kimokeo and whales.

The water dragon continued. "It was not by accident that you and Kimokeo met. Kimokeo has 75 percent Hawaiian blood, which is rare today, and even though you don't know your Hawaiian lineage, we brought you together because we are ancestors to you both. Ask Kimokeo to talk more about his experiences and what the elders say about us."

Taking the assignment seriously, later I phoned Kimokeo. Sharing my experience with the moʻo, I asked, "When I first met you, I felt you had a relationship with the whale? Is this true as well?"

"Yes, I do," Kimokeo answered. "It is a relationship with an *ʻaumakua* (ancestral guardian), like a guardian angel."

"When I spoke to the moʻo, it said it was one of your ʻaumakua. Do you feel this is true?"

"Yes I do," Kimokeo replied. "I have several connections to the moʻo. The moʻo Kiawahine is the guardian of the fishponds. I have never spoken to moʻo Kiawahine but know her presence in our *loko ia* (pond). Many times you don't need to speak—but just feel the presence, the spirit, of something."

"I feel this is why we have this kinship—because we both have this same ʻaumakua (ancestral guardian)," I replied.

I was grateful that Kimokeo took time from his busy days to speak with me about the moʻo. Being Hawaiian, he would be a much better choice to convey her words. I struggled with feelings of inadequacy and decided to ask the moʻo an obvious question.

"I understand the many things Kimokeo is doing for you, but why have you chosen to speak with me?" I asked.

"I speak to you because you can hear and speak with us. We moʻo wish you to share our message with humans…that all waters are sacred. Remember, your human body is composed mostly of water and without water you are dead. So protect the water!"

"I have spoken of this often and will continue to do so, however I'm curious about your origins."

"We are an old and proud race. Long ago we came from the stars, from the constellation you refer to as Draconis. The great Cosmic Dragon who births planets, and who is presently birthing Earth into a higher frequency, is our ancestor, even as we are the ancestors of dragon hybrids living in human form. Dragons are masters of all four elements: earth, air, fire, and water. We ocean moʻo concentrate our energy mostly on the water element, as do all moʻo, even land dwelling moʻokane. You must have noticed that the moʻokane of the dunes dwell beside the ocean; those in Kokee live in the mist covered higher reaches; and other moʻokane live alongside the Wailua River.

We are particularly strong on Kauai as it has more water than the Big Island where Pele rules. We are the energy that moves through the water, the consciousness in the water. Also—and this is important—although I dwell in Hawaii, other water dragons look after the waters in their countries and many humans have a lineage to us. We ancestors exist in the collective consciousness of all countries and speak to individuals through dreams, myths, and—if they devote the time—personal contact."

With those final words, the moʻo submerged and flowed back into the upwelling ocean. I've always thought that air and fire, not water, were my strengths, so I was confused about what I had in common with a water dragon. Rejoining Danny and Simon, I was unsettled as I told them of my powerful experience.

"I'd like to take you to meet another mo'o at the Waikapalae Wet Cave," said Danny, after he had bandaged my bloody leg. "They obviously want you to tell their story."

That meant ascending the cliff, which, fortunately, turned out to be less terrifying than the descent. Piling into the car, Danny donned his sandals and we drove to the cave, another sacred site for Hawaiians. Upon entering the cool cave, the three of us began to speak in hushed tones. A deep feeling of peace and of being watched pervaded this place. Made from a lava tube when Kauai was still forming, the cave contains a pristine, tranquil pool of turquoise-tinged water fed by underground springs that empty into the ocean.

As at the Dragon's Breath, I drew apart from my companions and awaited communication from the being I sensed lived there. Within minutes, a large white water dragon arose from the depths and swam unhurriedly towards me. My first impression was that it was blind, but my misunderstanding soon became apparent.

"I can choose to see or not see," the mo'o said, rolling a flap back from her eyes and staring fixedly at me. "I like to keep my eyes closed so I can enter a dream state in resonance with the Earth. I prefer to listen to the heartbeat of the Earth and to feel what we in Hawaii call 'aloha', rather than interact with humans who come here. Haole might think of me as a hermit, but Hawaiians regard me as an ancestor. I am a kahuna, a wisdom teacher of the mo'o."

The mo'o began to imprint me with the power of her thoughts and I opened to receive the energy this great being was sending.

The energy of the moʻo was very connected to ancient memories of the moʻo race and its relationship with the Earth. The moʻo kahuna spoke from the collective conscious of all life and most of what transpired between us was non-verbal. I intuited that this wise aumakua downloaded my astral body with information I could access at a later time, and in the way the ancestors wished. It wasn't only information that the moʻo gave me; in some ways it felt like glue—linkages to tie together the pieces of wisdom I'd been receiving previously from the menehune and moʻokane. The moʻo simultaneously gave me the task to bring this wisdom back into human consciousness.

Finished, the moʻo withdrew her energy, making clear that she didn't want to be disturbed further. With a telepathic prayer of gratitude, I removed my link to her and, still partially in the higher realms, reflected on how to fulfill the wishes that both the ocean and cave moʻo had requested. The life-force energy of both water dragons was so much stronger than either the menehune or moʻokane, which proved to me—as no words could—that the moʻo really were lesser gods, ancient ancestors. Danny startled me back to my physical body by speaking.

"If you still have energy, I'd like to take you to a special heiau (temple) nearby. It has been the most sacred site for hula for 90 generations of Hawaiians and, even today, it's a pilgrimage site for people who practice hula."

Already full from these two meetings with moʻo and my growing feelings of responsibility to convey their messages, I could have called it a day without adding anything more. However, I felt called to say "yes" to whatever Danny suggested and, being a keen fan of hula, Danny's idea was too tempting to refuse. Although

I've never taken lessons, I have fantasies about being able to do hula and do it WELL.

Not having heard of the Kaula o Laka Heiau, I became anxious when Danny parked at the entrance to the Na Pali Coast Trail. Oh no, I thought to myself, remembering my two grueling hikes on it.

What a relief to hear Danny say, "We're not embarking on the Na Pali trail, but are following a parallel one, a shorter one, nearer the beach."

Reassured, I commenced walking behind Danny. Before long the vista opened to a large, flat grassed-area where a heiau overlooked the sea. Unlike the abandoned heiaus I'd visited, this one still actively served its sacred purpose and great peace emanated from it.

Leis of fragrant flowers and green ti-leaves covered the rocks that formed a natural altar. Candles and small stone gifts accompanied these offerings. Unlike other heiaus where it was kapu to enter, I felt that all who were respectful were welcome here. This hula heiau radiated the true spirit of *aloha*. Often translated to mean "hello", "goodbye", or "love", aloha's deeper meaning is "the joyful sharing of life energy".

Seeking a blessing in this blissful place, I walked slowly to the altar where singing a song or saying a prayer, as well as leaving a lei, are all recognized as gifts. My openhearted prayer was a blessing on hula and on all those who bring such grace and beauty into the world. Furthermore, I prayed to convey the true Hawaiian spirit through the words that the mo'o and menehune were asking me to share with others. Finished, I looked up from my prayers to see a gentle, grandmother face beaming approval from the stone above me. Laka, the goddess of hula, was the ancestor receiving and blessing my prayers.

Withdrawing from the altar, my heart throbbing with love, I sat beside Danny. He showed me a photo that he'd taken of me praying. Grandmother's face was obvious to anyone looking at the photo. Turning to the altar to see her face again, I observed my leprechaun friend offering a ti-leaf lei to the grandmother. He was devotedly praying and doing exactly what he must have seen me do. I expected Lloyd to share his experiences after he finished, but he solemnly avoided my eyes. Respecting his space, I withdrew my attention from him and witnessed both Simon and Danny seek a blessing from the grandmother. Following our communication with her, we sat in silence allowing Laka's blessing to open our hearts more deeply to the spirit of aloha.

With sunset approaching, it was time to leave the Kaula o Laka Heiau. Danny broke the silence by saying, "I have a gift for you and the elementals. I've won awards for my chocolate treats and have made several delicacies to share. So Tanis, wait on the beach and enjoy the sunset; Simon, come and help me carry everything."

Danny is a man of many gifts. He's a guide, a professional photographer, and now I find out, a cook. Feeling like a queen— I could take a lot of this—I strolled onto the sandy beach.

Sunset and sunrise are my favorite times of the day. Hindu yogis say we can access spiritual realms easier during these times and I feel that to be true. I was meditating on the three powerful encounters I'd had this day, when I felt someone's energy nearby. Opening my eyes, I saw Lloyd gazing into the setting sun. We enjoyed silent companionship for some minutes before he spoke. "I wanted to join you earlier, but I've been very tied up with me study."

"You've been very close-mouthed about your study," I ventured, hoping he would say more.

"On these islands the moʻo, menehune, and ancestors are your teachers, me girl. Others are teaching me."

Not to be put off, I tried again, "What exactly are you learning?"

"Lots!" he answered, evading my question. My imagination leapt to the many things he could be doing, when he interrupted.

"Enough guessing. Here come the treats!" At that moment, Danny and Simon returned with their arms full of coconuts, flowers, puddings and homemade chocolate. Lloyd was predictably not in a hurry to depart once the treats had arrived. He and his elemental friends clustered around Danny to receive the beauty and aloha of his gifts. Although Danny and Simon did not see the elementals, both of them could sense their presence. Danny moved slowly and placed the food lovingly on a log. While Simon and I enjoyed eating our portions, the elementals absorbed the essence of Danny's bounty. We waited respectfully until they had finished before gathering up the remnants. A perfect end to a perfect day!

Young Menehune
Seek Human Partners

The next morning the sky was clear, a good day for a hike. Simon and I enjoyed walking in Waimea Canyon the year before, but we had only seen the upper section of Kokee. Waimea has diverse trails, so after consulting our map, we drove to the one with the waterfalls, always a first on our list.

We arrived at the trailhead and, getting out of the car, started walking. Because Lloyd had been absent for morning chats and adventures, I was astonished when he abruptly manifested on the path and took the lead. He wore a helmet, right out of Stanley and Livingston, the only difference being that his helmet sported shamrocks. His tree-limb hiking staff was adorned with leaves and flowers resembling the fertility pole of a May Day celebration. He had no words for me; just forged ahead at a good pace taking it for granted that I would keep up. I could think of only one reason for the hurry—we would be meeting menehune or moʻokane soon. It was not unexpected then, when a contingent of menehune blocked the path as we rounded the next bend.

An elf-like menehune with soft, coffee-colored skin stepped forward. He was bare-chested, clad with forest-green leaves woven around his waist, and his proud brow was crowned with a lei of matching leaves. In the traditional manner of a male speaking to another male, he addressed Lloyd.

"We have a large community of menehune living in Kokee and Waimea. There are only a few trails here, so not many humans disturb us. We know our brothers and sisters in the upper forest of Kokee greeted you with a ceremony of 'awa' (kava drink), so you are now our kin as well. We welcome you and your female partner to our community."

Lloyd and I remained motionless while he spoke and, when he finished, he moved forward and touched his forehead to Lloyd's, and then to mine as we shared the breath of aloha.

Stepping back, he continued, "We have a request. Word of your work helping elementals to partner with humans to create a beautiful and healthy Earth has reached us, and certain members of our community wish to join. We know you prefer mature elementals in your group, but we urge you to accept some of our younger menehune. We believe the young ones, with their open minds, will acquire knowledge more quickly from human partners and this will benefit our entire community."

Lloyd seemed anxious. Excusing himself, he turned to me with a concerned look on his face, "I have me reservations about this. Even older, stronger elementals have trouble partnering with humans, so we don't know if these young 'uns can maintain themselves in such partnerships. Because they aren't yet formed, their real essence may be obliterated."

"Is there any way we can agree to this request and still keep the young ones safe?" I asked Lloyd, deferring to his greater wisdom in matters dealing with elementals and menehune.

"Only if they partner in tribes," he responded, stroking his chin. "Many small ones together could be adopted by one human. That way, the energy of the human would not overwhelm them."

Overhearing our conversation, the menehune spokesperson jumped in to accept the leprechaun's suggestion, "We ask you to look for mothering humans, who will be gentle and not overpower our little ones. We want our children to keep their innocence. Please find good-hearted humans who are not fixed in their thoughts and who love to play."

Turning my attention toward the group, I noticed many childlike menehune of both genders attentively listening. They seemed to understand what their commitment would mean and one little male, dressed like a miniature version of the elf-like menehune, stepped forward to speak.

"We've been studying humans, so we understand. Because we can travel in space and time, we'll be able to spend some time with our family here in the forest and some time with our human. This way we'll not have to be with our human all the time. If we're in danger of getting lost in the human world, we can depend on our elders to call us home. We want to be menehune, after all."

With those words, the little male retreated into his peer group, as the elder menehune beamed proudly. This must be his child, I thought. At that moment, my attention was drawn to a female aliʻi elder, obviously a human ancestor, standing off to one side and witnessing our interaction.

Regal and dwarfing all of us in size, she wore a cloak of luminescent yellow and red feathers and carried a feather baton. Like previous occasions, this ancestor spoke neither to me, nor Lloyd, nor to the menehune. Still, I felt certain that if this ancestor didn't agree, no agreement would be reached between us. As these thoughts flickered through my mind, a sudden warmth descended over me signaling that the ancestor bestowed her approval. My heart expanded with greater love, for I knew she trusted us with the children.

Lloyd must have had the same feeling because he moved closer and merged his energy with mine. The moment we did this, the community surrounded us, allowing us to radiate our combined energies to them and, in return, they radiated their combined energy to us. Like exchanges in blood transfusions, we can send our life energy to another through thought and willpower and this will change them. Receiving energy from another happens the same way. Lloyd stood solemnly engaged in this process. Our energy exchange was an unspoken commitment to the menehune to keep their children safe.

Our ritual complete, the community disappeared as quickly as they had come. Before I could say anything, Lloyd raised his hand to stop me, "It's good what we've accomplished, but I don't have time to chat right now. I'm very busy training and getting ready and time is pressing."

"For what?" I was able to interject into his dissolving form.

"You'll see soon enough," I heard echoing from the ethers.

Lloyd has an acute sense of timing, and is loyal to his inner guidance.

To give me privacy, Simon had wandered ahead on the path when I stopped to speak with the menehune and I found him sitting on a log around the next bend enjoying the forest's peaceful silence. Joining him we silently continued hiking through the forest to a breathtaking waterfall that falls hundreds of feet to the canyon floor. While Simon ventured closer to the edge to explore the various drops in the waterfall, I sat further back to think. My thoughts kept wandering back to the continual, not so subtle, hints the leprechaun had made several times about training that kept him so busy. Obviously, I was supposed to get it, but what was "it"? The answer was soon to arrive.

One of the highlights of my visit to Kauai the previous year was attending an evening in celebration of hula. I love the grace and beauty of hula and find it the softest, most gentle expression of femininity in dance. When I was young, perhaps eight or nine, my father's cousin Elmer, who had lived in Hawaii most of his life, came to visit. We lived in a subdivision in a small town where hockey reigned supreme. No graceful dance to be found there. It was a magical evening when Cousin Elmer demonstrated a few hula hand movements. I practiced the movements for years afterwards in the privacy of my bedroom.

Imagine my joy to know that this hula evening was an annual event and, by coincidence, we had returned to Kauai at the correct time to attend. I had the perfect dress. My mother had an elderly friend, Margarite, whom I met only once before her passing. But on that occasion, she went to her bedroom and returned carrying an antique Hawaiian muumuu-like dress.

"I was in Hawaii when I was a young woman," Margarite said. "I've had this dress since then and I want you to have it."

The dress is lovely and made up of several orange, yellow, and mustard-colored floral panels. Sky-blue and brown are thrown in for contrast and a lovely fringe trims the bottom. Hand-made with natural dyes, I think. When I wear it, which is NEVER in Canada, I receive compliments. This dress feels like hula, like ancient days in Hawaii, and it helps me awaken the deep, feminine energies that have been slumbering in my life.

That evening, after returning from Waimea, was the hula event. Freshly showered and decked out in the dress, I entered the auditorium with my date. Simon prefers not to be too close to the stage as loud sounds bother him, so he headed for a couple of seats in the middle. We had no sooner sat down than a large woman with bouffant hair parked herself in front of me. Looking around for an alternative, I was drawn to two seats in the second row close to the stage and Simon understood. All the better to see the performers and the right location, as it turned out, for a synchronicity to happen!

On the previous day, saying goodbye to Danny, I'd asked if he knew any kumu (teachers) who might know more about the mysterious mo'o. Danny mentioned that it might be helpful to speak with a certain Hawaiian woman, a kumu who was an expert in Hawaiian culture. He called to see if she would meet with me, but she said she was too busy. Could it be an accident, therefore, to find myself in an auditorium filled with hundreds of people sitting directly behind a regal Hawaiian woman who is addressed by the same unique name by the woman sitting next to me? Believing this to be a sign from the universe, I requested an introduction.

"Hello, I'm Tanis Helliwell, the woman Danny Hoshimoto called you about," I said.

"Pleased to meet you," she replied politely, and then quickly looked away.

Disappointed, I accepted the fact that she did not want to speak with me. I could not understand, when the signs supporting our meeting seemed clear, she had closed the door. It was only later I discovered that her expertise was in traditional Hawaiian crafts. Perhaps, I surmised, she wasn't an expert in moʻo and, for that reason, didn't feel she had anything to share. Or was it because I was a haole, a foreigner, that she didn't feel comfortable talking about moʻo? In any event, I accepted the dismissal and had faith that the ancestors would assist me in their time. The synchronicity of being seated behind this striking woman renewed my confidence that the ancestors were showing the way. They had also gifted me by bringing me closer to the hula dancers.

Reading up on hula to better appreciate what I was seeing, I discovered that there are two types of hula. While Simon and I waited for the event to start, I shared what I had learned with him.

"Did you know that Hula Kahiko is the traditional form of temple dance originally performed for the gods? Hula Kahiko was linked to the kāhuna sending spiritual energies, mana, to the gods to ask for strength and protection. And some Hula Kahiko honored the aliʻi, because they were thought to be descended from the gods."

"Is that the kind we're seeing tonight?" asked Simon.

"I don't know yet," I replied. "But I do know that everything associated with hula was originally done with ritual and respect including choosing the plants, making the leis, prayers preceding the performance, and disposal of the leis afterwards. There is mana in the words, in the precision of the performance, and in the harmony of the dancer's movements and, even a minor error, could invalidate the message to the gods and bring bad luck. Hawaiians didn't have a written language and hula was their way of recording their legends, genealogies, and history. Every gesture in hula has a specific meaning and chants accompany the movements to tell the story. The first time hula was performed in public was 1886 when King Kalakaua, who called hula 'the language of the heart', gave his permission."

"Is this the kind of hula I like?" asked Simon, hoping to see some relevance in what I was sharing.

"The kind of hula you like is a new form. It is called Hula Auana and, instead of being performed with the traditional instruments of drums and rattles, it's performed with modern instruments of ukulele, double bass, and slack-key guitar, which I know you love."

At the moment the lights dimmed and the celebration started. A revered woman kumu, who we had seen the previous year, entered accompanied with people whose instruments showed that they were going to perform—unfortunately for Simon—mostly traditional hula. Groups of women and children performed first, and the time arrived for the men to do their version of the hula. Traditionally, men dance a different kind of hula than women. Men need a combination of both athletic strength and flowing grace, blending yang and yin qualities together. They usually start as boys, then dedication and long study are required to attain the combination.

A large group of men entered the stage. All were dressed in green ti-leaves circling their waists and with leis on their heads, necks, wrists, and ankles. From their dress, it looked to me, the uninitiated, as if they would perform Hula Kahiko and I was looking forward to their performance. One moment he wasn't there and the next moment he was. You know who I mean. Standing in the back row behind big men, and dressed exactly like them, was a short, red-haired leprechaun with large feet. I couldn't believe my eyes and held my breath hoping against hope that a disaster was not about to occur.

The kumu began chanting prayers for the hula and the dancers remained motionless. Next, the dancers chanted words that preceded the hula and I saw my friend mouthing the right words. So far, so good. The dancers commenced the dance and flowed in harmony. My eyes were glued to the dancer in the back row and I sent continuous prayers to Laka, the goddess of hula, for a flawless ceremony. Quick stamping steps from right to left with arms accompanying these steps—and the leprechaun was keeping up. All went incredibly well through the first number and I breathed a sigh of relief. Surely now he would have the good sense to remove himself from the stage. Not so.

The dancers dropped to their knees and the kumu began the chant for the second hula. There was Lloyd staring fixedly and primed to continue. While tapping on their knees and the floor, the men moved seamlessly together and, praise be to Laka, my friend did, too. I finally understood how seriously he was taking his role. After the hula came to an end, he grinned with self-pleasure and rose with the other men. When the dancers exited the stage, the one in front of Lloyd, glanced towards him, then made room for my friend to pass.

Quite a night and I could hardly wait to congratulate Lloyd the next time I saw him.

Blessings by the Ancestors
at the Hoʻopiʻi Falls

Nights passed sleeping under the stars overlooking Prince Kuhio Park. I didn't visit the ancestors there again since the time didn't feel right. It felt like I was being readied for something, as more menehune and moʻokane taught me until, drop-by-drop, my vessel was full enough for a leap in learning, or a change in consciousness. Questions still prodded me concerning the role of ancestors and their reason for contacting me, but neither Lloyd, nor they, seemed willing to answer them. My leprechaun friend was absent for days, a relief in some ways, now I could enjoy time with Simon. However, in other ways, I felt lost in an unknown land without a map.

Then a breakthrough occurred. While awaking one morning on the lanai, the elusive leprechaun showed up. Pulling up a chair, he plopped himself down and took a deep gulp from a steaming cup of black tea. He had no trouble manifesting it in the etheric realm where he could drink his tea, but he always liked me to provide tea in the physical world, so he could absorb the essence.

"Is there one for me?" I joked.

"Only if you make it, me dear. I haven't found a way yet to bring you tea in bed."

"I'm sure it can wait. I'm happy to see you and haven't had the chance to congratulate you on your astounding hula performance," I said, pulling myself into a sitting position.

"Oh, but you did. I heard your prayers during me hula and knew you were pulling for me. We're bonded and, when you send such strong thoughts, it would be difficult to keep from hearing them."

"Well then, you know I have several questions seeking answers. For instance, what have you been studying and why did you keep it secret?"

"I've been fulfilling me commitment as an honorary kahuna and that means training in ceremony, rituals, and hula. Of course, I'll never be very good at hula 'cos I've started way too late, but I'm dedicated and sit in on as many practices as I can. Men and women traditionally have their own study path and they keep the teachings secret from one another, so I couldn't discuss it with you. Added to that, I'm still a haole and have to try extra hard to observe the kapu."

"Amazing. Just how long have you been studying? And why, with all the other cultural traditions you could have chosen, did you commit to the Hawaiian?"

"Two questions, but I'll be lenient this time. You've been patient with me not being around to talk to about menehune and mo'okane; therefore you deserve some patience from me. So…I'm studying the Hawaiian tradition, 'cos the old elementals that are me teachers and ancestors thought I needed to be more yin, more accepting, less assertive. Can you imagine?"

"It's been going on four years now and I pop over here whenever I get free time away from helping elementals to find human partners. The mo'okane, menehune, and ancestors have chosen to teach you their traditions to awaken memories from your Hawaiian lives. Being a kahuna in former lives, the memory pattern lives in your body elemental, your etheric body, for all of them to see.

"All of us unseen beings, as you like to say, live in different realms in the astral world. Because our frequencies are closer together than those of humans who are only conscious in the physical world, we can see, hear, and walk in each other's world. Well, not exactly ALL of us. Should be a bit more specific. Kahuna or ali'i of both menehune and humans have more mana (spiritual power), so they can visit and even live in each other's realms."

"I would like to know ..." I said.

"Nope. Don't interrupt. I don't want to lose me train of thought 'cos you need to know what I'm telling you."

Quick to take his long-sought advice, I stayed quiet.

"I know what you're going to ask, so let's put you out of your misery. Here's the piece of cheese you hoped for." Lloyd projected an image of a tiny mouse with my face begging a beneficent him.

"Humans on the spiritual path can visit these astral realms to communicate with the many kinds of beings who live there. In fact, all humans will master this in your so-called Aquarian Age. The next two thousand years, that is. Not to puff you up, but you've a bit of a head start in this area. That's why the various kāhuna have been eager to share their knowledge with you. And it's your sacred responsibility to pass on this information. The first step to encounter the astral realm is to believe in it and in the various beings who live there. This way individuals can set up their own links with their ancestors to get answers to their own questions.

"Any MORE questions?" he crossed his arms across his plump chest and dared me to find one.

"I appreciate what these wonderful beings are sharing with me and treasure their trust, however I'd love confirmation from Hawaiians, humans that is, and have singularly struck out in that regard," I stated and then pushed a bit further. "And I'd still like to know more about the role of ancestors, especially in my life."

"Don't worry! It's coming in Hawaiian time and in a Hawaiian way. Why don't you take a little trip to the museum in Lihue?" he said, dangling another piece of cheese, as he waved farewell.

Ready to act on his hint, I went inside to get Simon up. Can't understand why he'd rather sleep in a bed when he could dream under the stars in a sleeping bag like me. After eating some porridge—and leaving enough for Lloyd should he return—we drove to the museum. Simon loves tools so he was happy to examine their collection, while I went searching for information on mo'o.

Looking through the bookstore, I found a few books with folk tales about menehune. But other than a few legends, there was nothing about individuals talking with mo'o, and the mo'okane weren't mentioned at all. Approaching the Hawaiian curator, I asked, "Do you have any literature relating to actual meetings with mo'o?"

"No, I don't," she replied. She was polite and smiling, however I felt an unwillingness to reveal any more to a haole. I've encountered a similar reluctance in Ireland where the Irish don't want to discuss leprechauns. Perhaps locals feel they'll be mocked, if they believe in elementals and mythic beings.

Wondering about mentioning my experiences, I decided on a circuitous route.

"I was speaking with Kimokeo Kapahulehu on Maui about the menehune and other beings found in folklore. He is from Kauai… do you happen to know him?"

Her smile broadened and the door opened, "Oh, yes, he is the brother of my good friend and we expect him back for a visit soon."

"This might sound crazy, but here goes. For the past four years, I've met many menehune and mo'o and they want me to write about what they're telling me. Consequently, I want to check the accuracy of these experiences."

"That's wonderful and we would love a copy of anything you write," she replied, exuding a new openness and trust.

"If you know anyone I could speak to or anywhere to go, I'd appreciate knowing."

"Sorry, but I have no information I think would help."

This warm woman was forthcoming and I had attempted to do the research. If Spirit, mo'o, and ancestors wished me to know more, they would tell me in their time.

Luckily, I didn't have long to wait. That same afternoon I was teaching a course that included an excursion into a fairy forest. Although the excursion was advertised to meet elementals, I've noticed the universe gives you exactly what it wants, regardless of your expectations.

I shared stories about my adventures with the menehune and moʻo, and the participants were eager to have their own experiences. I was keen, too, because it was the first time I'd visited this enchanted forest and the Hoʻopiʻi Falls. Ready to depart, we first stopped at the forest entrance to give thanks for the gift of its beauty and life and to pray for openness to receive elementals and any others who wanted to meet us.

No sooner had we started along the trail than Lloyd arrived and, without stopping to speak, moved to the front of the line. He made it clear by his solemn face that we were to remain in silence. In his hand, he carried a large koʻokoʻo, his walking staff, the kind the royal aliʻi carry, and I assumed he'd been given this as a token of his acceptance by the aliʻi. The staff was taller than him, but he had no trouble stepping forward with purpose, like a drum major in a marching band. I sensed our human group was the main attraction.

My intuition was confirmed right away when a procession of menehune and moʻokane appeared, walking quietly in single file behind us. Some I'd met before in Kauai, but it was the first time for others, which I knew intuitively had come from all the Hawaiian Islands. Sending whispered questions about their purpose in their direction, I received back, likewise in whispers, the words, "The ancestors have called us to heal their wounds and those of the Earth."

"What wounds?" I telepathically whispered.

"The suffering of the Hawaiian people and the lack of respect for their traditions by the invaders," I heard back while the leprechaun sent me a stronger "not now" message to be silent.

Slowly our descent opened up into a magical, fairy forest full of moss-covered, sentient trees observing our progress. Unseen forces commanded me to veer off the path to the left and, when I did, Lloyd followed. I signaled our group to make a circle beside three old trees in a secluded spot by the river. The moment we seated ourselves, a rooster crowed, began walking towards us and, like a guard, posted himself behind our backs. The cock crowed a second time announcing that some momentous event was about to begin. Lloyd and his friends moved into place and formed a sacred ring around us to observe our proceedings.

The conscious trees and other beings of the forest emitted peace and unconditional love. All of us knew we had entered a realm outside of time and space. In the sacred atmosphere the old trees created, I listened to uncover what was asked of us, and heard that each of us was to speak from our hearts, with aloha, about what we felt Spirit and the ancestors were calling us to do.

The first person to speak was an expert in earth healing who had written a book on this topic.

"I wish to help the people I meet in the resort where I work to become aware of the sacred aspects of the Hawaiian culture," she shared. The rest of us visualized her accomplishing her goal.

A graceful, generous-hearted woman healer went next. "I want to make a bigger home for the Heart of Kauai for all people to live in joy."

We continued sharing and the last person to share was a quiet man who believed in elementals. He stated, "My passion is walking in nature and I do it every chance I get, but I'm always alone and would like to go with others. Also, I feel the presence of elementals when I'm in nature, but have never seen them and would love to. One more thing. I'm not clear about what I can do to help the Earth."

After each of us had prayed for guidance and shared what we had received, I opened myself further to discover what the beings in this sacred place were asking us to do next. Immediately, a group of royal ali'i and kāhuna ancestors advanced from the river. I hadn't seen them until that moment and realized that they could choose to be seen, or unseen. Among them were the royal guards from Prince Kuhio's heiau, the mo'okane from the Wailua River, and the elf-like menehune and female ali'i who had sponsored the menehune children in Waimea. And that's not all: Burt and Daisy had come, too.

As the ancestors began to approach, the old trees created an etheric heiau, forming a protective dome of light over and around us. The ancestors began to beam a broad, full-hearted aloha to us. Their blessing was because of the work we were doing to love and serve the Earth. The powerful energy resembled the sun's energy and I could feel it passing through us to anchor Spirit on the Earth.

Dressed in a flowing blue and white muumuu, a barefoot Daisy stepped forward revealing her real self. This was a deeper, more authoritative Daisy than I had encountered previously. Lives of wisdom flicked across her face, gifting me with levels of her being. I realized that she'd called herself "Daisy" to illustrate the various aspects of her existence, even as a daisy has many separate petals making up one blossom.

"We've been preparing you for this moment," Daisy spoke to me. "These humans live in Kauai. They love and are committed to this land. Even so, we have been preparing them energetically for many years to accept our teachings. You, on the other hand, are a haole, an outsider, so we asked the menehune and mo'okane to teach you over these last years to ready you for us. Our teachings are not only by words, but through experiences, opportunities, and people we send your way. The language of the heart, or aloha, is wordless and this is what we offer all of you now."

Lloyd chose that moment to step forward from the outer circle. Leis, from each place he had been gifted, hung around his neck. Evidently, he'd been preparing for this moment as well.

Addressing him, Daisy said, "We're happy with the work you do with the elementals around the world seeking to partner with humans. Some elemental individuals now have enough mana and wisdom both to learn from and to teach the menehune and mo'okane we have sent you. Also, because you've been studying our Hawaiian traditions, you're a bridge from us to the elemental realms."

Turning back towards me, she continued, "We're happy with your partnership with the elementals since it's a model for us of a modern way. We ancestors keep the Hawaiian traditions pure and strong for our descendants and for the mana of this 'aina (land).

Some ancestors on the Islands, like ancestors in other countries, want to maintain the purity of these traditions, while others, like us, want to lend our energy to the new way, to help humans of the present day who wish to work with the menehune, elementals, and ancestors. This is why we are speaking with you now.

"Often your path and ours are the same, Tanis." This was the first time Daisy had spoken my name and her doing so had a profound effect. I felt deeply seen and was moved almost to tears.

"For example, you led tours to sacred sites of the Earth for 20 years. You did this to increase the mana of the Earth and the pilgrims. In olden times, kāhuna took Hawaiians on pilgrimages to the sacred heiaus for the same reasons. Because your motivation and ours are the same, we are opening our eyes to new ways of sharing and healing."

Daisy stepped back into her group at the same time as the female ali'i ancestor who had protected the children in Waimea stepped forward. She was much taller than me and wore a beautiful yellow, red, and black feathered cloak around her shoulders. From her bearing, this ali'i ancestor must be a princess or queen. Walking regally towards the mo'okane and menehune who surrounded us, she touched each of them on top of their heads with a blessing. She then moved towards us humans where, bending over, she shared the traditional Hawaiian greeting of placing her nose and forehead against ours individually and sharing her breath. Staring intently into my eyes, I felt her energetically catalyze me to be a bridge to non-Hawaiian peoples and to share the Hawaiian wisdom as best I could. She and the other ancestors did not doubt me, and they did not want me to doubt myself. Also, I intuited that the breath we shared with her, would in turn be breathed into the ancestors and the kāhuna who guard all of Kauai.

As she stepped back into the group of ancestors, an immense mo'o emerged from the river and approached us. Out of water, it physically resembled its close dragon relatives while exuding compassion, strength, and protection. I knew its intentions, even as I understood the purpose of the rituals with the other ancestors. It was also clear that the mo'o wished me to be its voice.

Speaking to our human group, I shared, "The mo'o have been here since Lemurian times and Hawaii, like other Polynesian Islands, still embody the essence of Lemuria. Its' soft, yin, nurturing emotional nature has been undervalued in our solar, yang, mental western world. The mo'o want to reawaken these qualities in each of us and convey to others through their story the importance, if we want to be sane and healthy, of reawakening these energies in our world. This moʻo wishes to enshroud us in the mist of this earlier era on Kauai. She is giving us her etheric energy, her mana, and her memory of the eons that the moʻo have protected the waters here. I am saying 'she', however, in most ways the moʻo think of themselves as genderless. The word 'it' is inappropriate because it may incline you to think less of the moʻo, as if she were a thing, not the great being she is."

As the moʻo approached to share the mist of her memories, a physical mist descended from the sky to bless us. She embraced us in the dew of her essence and, completing her task, withdrew into the river. As quickly as they had arrived, the ancestors, menehune, and moʻokane left. The sentient trees removed the dome of light, the etheric heiau, from around us and the rooster, which had guarded our back, departed.

Awed and humbled by what had transpired, our group wanted to give something back. We wandered through the mystical forest to the Hoʻopiʻi Falls to happily spread the joy and aloha of the profound blessing we had received.

The Place of Refuge
on The Big Island

Because Kauaians hold more ceremonies to chant, dance, pray, and listen to the ancestors, Hawaiians refer to Kauai as being the most spiritual of the Islands. For this reason it was with a heavy heart that I left Kauai for the Big Island. Although I didn't feel drawn to the Big Island, Spirit evidently had other plans. When friends invited Simon and I to visit them and a public talk was organized for me, we committed to go. It felt necessary, as if something was sleeping in the darkness that would awaken there.

It could not have been more fitting that we started our visit at one of the most sacred places on the Big Island, Puʻuhonua o Honaunau, also known as the place of refuge. Located on the west coast in a sheltered bay with plenty of drinking water, it was a natural place for the aliʻi to establish one of their most important residences. Here the chiefs of the Kona district engaged in negotiating war or peace, in playing a Hawaiian board game resembling checkers called *konane*, and in riding wooden sleds down the mountainside. Servants performed daily tasks, such as making pots, clothes, and cooking.

Hawaiians are a large people. Westerners recorded both male and female ali'i as being over six feet tall and, according to oral tradition, in ancient times they were a foot or two taller than that. Keeping their mana—life force—strong and pure was of primary importance to ancient Hawaiians. Even today one's lineage is important in Hawaii. In order to keep their mana strong, the king or queen, like the ancient Egyptians, sometimes married a close relative, or relatives. This did not endear them to Christian missionaries who were unable to understand the spiritual significance of keeping the mana strong within a lineage. It is interesting, therefore, that the missionaries did not destroy Pu'uhonua o Honaunau and that it still exists hundreds of years after it was built.

Starting to walk through the site, I heard royal ali'i ancestors speaking to me from afar, "We welcome you here. Allow the sacred energy of this place to rekindle memories of your Hawaiian lives."

While Simon headed for the fishpond to see how it worked, I was drawn to a massive stonewall that separated the royal grounds from Pu'uhonua o Honaunau. Entering the enclosure where the place of refuge is located, I came upon an ancient temple, a heiau that radiated power. It was built on a power site of the Earth where it accessed the mana both of Spirit from above and Earth from below. The bones of many powerful ali'i had resided in this heiau and Hawaiians believed the mana from the bones gave this site power. I could feel that power streaming down from the extant heiau that still existed in the astral world.

At one time, there were many places of refuge and individuals could go to the nearest one for safety. In sanctuaries such as this, enemies and those who had broken kapu were given a second chance. It was kapu, for example, for commoners to let their shadow fall on the king, for women to eat with men, and to eat food reserved for the gods. There were strictly controlled seasons for fishing, killing animals, and gathering timber and it was kapu to do any of these outside certain times.

If individuals broke these, or other, taboos their spouses, children or parents reported them because, if they didn't, they would be in danger themselves. This meant that the accused individuals had to run or swim to a place of refuge to save their lives. Also, women, children, sick, and elderly would go to a place of refuge and be safe while the warriors fought battles. Blood could not be shed within the walls of a place of refuge. If an individual got to one, a kahuna would do a purification ceremony after which the refugee could return home. The system, although harsh, worked well for many hundreds of years and established law in Hawaii. When King Kamehameha II outlawed the Hawaiian religion in the 1800s, more than six months before the arrival of the first Christian missionaries, all the heiaus and places of refuge, except for Pu'uhonua o Honaunau, were destroyed.

The site was fascinating and the only one I had visited that gave a real sense of what living in Hawaii had been like in ancient days. After meditating and walking around the grounds, I went to an introduction given by the ranger, Kale Hua, who has worked at Pu'uhonua o Honaunau for decades. Listening to his talk, I knew he was a spiritual man and a guardian of this sacred place. After he finished, I went to speak with him.

"Is this site still used for spiritual purposes?" I inquired.

"People come here and leave gifts," Kale Hua said. "Some leave whisky, others a stone, and one person left a can of Spam. Following tradition, I remove the gifts, but I wouldn't remove the Spam because it might have been the guy's last can."

He was well informed about spiritual practices at this site, and I wondered if he knew anything about the moʻo. Tripping over my tongue in my eagerness not to offend, I began, "I'm continually meeting moʻo and other ancestors and it's difficult finding Hawaiians who will speak to me about this and I want to be sure I'm on the right track."

"The moʻo is a family guardian angel," Kale Hua replied, encouraging a conversation. "These guardians come in different forms and every family has one or two. They make connections with a family member and appear to you. They don't come to frighten or scare you, but to let you know they are there to protect you.

"I've been working here for over 30 years and sometimes I go into the back country to patrol. No one else wants to go except me and, if I see a light, I want to check it out. One time I saw a light around midnight. But when I arrived at the place there was no light. I had to walk two miles back in the dark. I could feel something following me and finally I saw it was an owl. The next day when I told my Dad about it, he was smiling.

"What's happening Dad?"

He said, "I never told you that our family has two guardian angels—the owl and the shark."

"From that time," said Kale Hua, "I always know I'm being watched, so I'm never scared here at night. It's the same for you.

You're being watched and protected by the mo'o."

"I feel protected and for some reason, they are communicating with me," I shared. "Originally, I thought my work was with humans. Then about 30 years ago, I met elementals who wanted me to tell their story, and now I'm meeting mo'o and ancestors who wish the same."

"You have a gift," said Kale Hua. "The mo'o could be protecting you because they want you to share this information with others. This could be your calling. Hawaiians didn't write things down; they just talked story. That was their way of sharing about their ancestral spirits. Hawaiians kept these visions within the family. Not that they were sacred, but they were meant for only their family."

"Did the kāhuna share this?" I asked.

"There were all kinds of kāhuna," Kale Hua said. "But one kind worked with magic and was a liaison between the spirit world and the real world."

"The veil between the worlds has always been thin for me."

"You are lucky because not many can say that. You need strength and mana to work with the spirits, so you can tell others what you saw, heard, and experienced."

Happy that a Hawaiian was sharing freely with me, I pursued another topic for clarification. "Do you think the menehune were the original people on the islands and that the Hawaiians pushed them away when they arrived?"

"I've always thought," he said, "that the original people, the menehune, came from the Marquises Islands. They were smaller in stature and they were industrious. When they had a project, like building fishponds, they had to finish it that night. The second migration was large people from Tahiti who brought the idea of sacrifice to their gods and they sacrificed these small people who were strong in spiritual power. After running out of menehune, they started sacrificing others."

At this moment, others wishing to talk to Kale Hua interrupted, so I thanked him and said goodbye. His words about family ancestors and his affirmations of what had been happening to me were a great comfort.

Months after speaking with Kale Hua, I was back home walking in the rain, when suddenly I had a flashback to a part of the conversation we had. I must have put it out of my mind because I wasn't prepared to see an unpleasant aspect of myself. There are depths in our unconscious where we are not aware; that only surface when we're ready. This is what happened:

"Is there anyone else I could speak with who might know something about the moʻo?" I asked.

"One of my friends is more spiritual than me and studying traditionally, but he's not well. I don't know if he'd speak with you," said Kale Hua.

"What's wrong with him? Maybe I can help."

"He thinks he's been cursed by someone and he's asked one of our healers to remove the curse, but he keeps getting worse."

"How ill?" I asked.

"Really ill. Kidney failure. He can't leave the house."

At that moment I realized I could do nothing. This was an area that I knew existed, but I didn't want to go there, although I felt great sympathy for the person. In our western culture, we delude ourselves into thinking that cursing another person to make them ill, or even kill them, is impossible. I have studied with enough Indigenous people to know that it is possible. In the modern world, this happens too, although not obviously. For example, if you think badly of a person, you actually harm him, and conversely, if you think well of that person, you send him energy. This is the power of thought. Each of us can do this and those with more power do it better than others.

There are warriors of power who want to steal power from others both in western and Indigenous worlds. It sounded as if one might have cursed Kale Hua's friend. I prefer to think of myself as a warrior of love and stay clear of the other path. However, that might not always have been the case because on a few occasions, when warriors of power have confronted me, I intuitively knew how to defend myself. Perhaps, in my former Hawaiian lives, Pele, the volcano goddess, taught me this. I was soon to find out!

Meeting Pele at
Volcanoes National Park

There are few stories about mo'o in Hawaiian myths, and the most often recounted tales speak of mo'o and Pele as antagonists. In one of these legends, Pele, the volcano goddess, sent her youngest sister, Hi'iaka, to rescue a mortal lover who was held hostage in a cave by three mo'o. On the way, Hi'iaka encounters many mo'o whom she defeats and kills.

Why are the water dragon mo'o and Pele enemies in these legends? This puzzled me. Could it be the natural incompatibility between the elements of water (mo'o) and fire (Pele)? Was it rivalry between two family groups who believed their rivalry stemmed from their two 'aumakua (ancestral guardians)? Kauai, where the mo'o reign, was created long before the Big Island, the home of Pele. So was their rivalry that of the younger child trying to prove she was better than the elder child, or a newer religion challenging an older one? Because mo'o were usually female and female ali'i often claimed the mo'o as their protector, was Pele, another female, jealous?

I wanted to understand if these possibilities explained the mythic antagonism. Pele's presence is strongest on the Big Island because several volcanoes are active there. And Hawaii Volcanoes National Park is reputed to be the place with the strongest connection to Pele, so that was the obvious place to go. In addition, the rainbow deva that I'd met at the secret falls had told me to contact Pele and I followed her guidance.

Simon and I had visited the park twice over the space of a week, but I'd received no invitation from Pele. On the third visit, this changed. Simon had gone ahead to the visitor's center where he could learn more about the geological formations—one of his loves—while I strolled along a path that had vents of steam coming out of the ground. That's when I heard her summons from deep inside the earth.

"Come, stand here!" Pele commanded, indicating a place near a steam vent where odors and poisonous sulfur fumes were spewing.

It wouldn't have been my first choice, but doing as she requested, I waited for her to continue.

"My ancestor is the Divine Cosmic Mother. So I am her, and she is me. We are One. As such, I am primeval. I originated in the earliest times. I am an aspect of the Egyptian goddess Sekhmet, who was both a creator and destroyer. Likewise, I am related to Kali, the Indian goddess of creation and destruction. My fire catalyzes sexuality, spirituality, creativity, and energy to do anything. Both women and men pray to me to help them accomplish their goals and, if they have too much water, they don't accomplish anything. Maintaining a balance of fire and water is the key to create and then nurture what you created. The steam from my vents is made up of both fire and water."

Hearing my unspoken question about her and the moʻo being enemies, she responded, "The moʻo are my sisters and their strength is on Kauai. I couldn't live there because I am too much fire, however I am happy that they are looking after the gardens and the water. My energy is to start things. Their energies are needed to continue. I create and destroy what is no longer needed so the energy can be used to create new things. I work with the Sun and fire elementals, salamanders by another name, to keep the Earth warm. These fire elementals are in my molten core and in my lava. They emerge when I breathe out through the steam vents, but they prefer to live in my molten lava."

"I appreciate you speaking about your positive relationship with the moʻo because the story that you were enemies didn't feel right to me," I said, unwilling to let go of that topic.

"Individuals interpret our relationship at the level of understanding they are at in their own life. As they evolve in consciousness, they access deeper levels of truth about us ancestors. How you relate to me has also evolved."

"I don't understand. I didn't think I had a relationship with you," I answered, nervous about what she might tell me.

"I am in charge of the kundalini fire, the life-force energy of the body. Because your central channel was somewhat blocked in younger years, my fire could not rise properly to your crown. This is why you ended up with second-degree burns on your skin until I could clear the blockages in your chakras. You will recall that your first major burn happened right here on the Big Island in 1986, when you were leading a retreat called the Circle of Creation. You unconsciously chose the name and theme of the retreat to reawaken your own kundalini, and you unconsciously invited me, your ancestor, to do this. I've been able to work actively in your physical, astral (emotional), and causal (mental) bodies since that time. Before that, I was working on more subtle levels."

Hearing her words, I remembered the burns and blisters I endured sporadically over much of my body for ten years. Many people who saw me thought I was on fire. Discovery Channel interviewed me twice about surviving spontaneous combustion. Not a pleasant period.

"But my fire, in addition to hurting you, also healed you," Pele said, softening her tone. "Do you remember taking the homeopathic remedy of sulfur, derived from my fire element, to heal your burns?"

"The sulfur did help, but I also recollect sitting for hours in baths trying to calm the fire. Would this be a gift from the mo'o?" I asked, feeling more drawn to the mo'o by the minute.

"It was, as was MY gift. The mo'o and I have been working with you for many lives, not only this one. Your strengths are in both fire and water. With fire, you lead others, pioneer new ideas, and move quickly. Your impatience with yourself and others, and saying harsh things without considering the consequences of your words are also fire. I have an affinity with you because of your fire. But you need to guard against speaking without first checking to see if your words could burn others."

Her severe appraisal shook me, but I sought to stay open and receptive to her words. Picking up on my self-critical thoughts, Pele volunteered, "Fire is the most dangerous element. It's not only what you personally need to change, but also what all people need to learn about fire.

"Think of the positive side of fire! Mother Earth births new land through me in Hawaii, Iceland, and other locations where there are live volcanoes. It takes hundreds of thousands of years, in human terms, to create earth and islands that will ultimately establish a habitation where plants, birds, and other beings can live, but fire begins this process."

"I've had a few years to get used to the idea that the moʻo are my ancestors," I said to her, "but it's overwhelming and confusing to learn in such a short time that you are my ancestor, too."

Impressing me with her thoughts, Pele continued. "You are fortunate that the moʻo are also your ancestors because water from the moʻo balances fire, my strength. From your mother, you received the moʻo ancestors and from your father, your lineage comes from me. Your father was solar, a self-starter, focused. You have devoted a great deal of this life following your father's lineage, which stems back to Atlantis and early Egypt. This is the solar, the fire path. My gifts have helped you achieve your goals in the outer world, to be successful in organizations. You are comfortable with command, are good at it, and even feel you deserve it. This comes from me through the aliʻi lineage in Hawaii.

"I feel the truth of what you're saying. But then, why have the moʻo, not you, been speaking to me for the past four years?" I asked.

"That's easy. You undervalue your mother's soft, yin nature and see it as weakness. Therefore, you undervalue her contribution to your lineage. But you used your mother's moʻo lineage as a psychotherapist, a seer, and healer of the Earth. Your mother was psychic, gifted with the second sight, as they say in Ireland— where you also have ancestors. Your mother's strength was lunar, based on emotions and water. Your kahuna (shaman) lineage in Hawaii comes from her. The moʻo contacted you to reawaken your mother's lineage. This lineage stems from Mu, ancient Lemuria, and the Hawaiian people and all Polynesians came from there. To Hawaiians, both ocean and ʻaina (land) are sacred and it's time for you to equally serve both ancestors: moʻo and me."

The force of her words struck me. Light burned through my shadowed areas to strip me naked, but in a good way. A freedom from restraints and convention emerged. Physical, emotional, and thought levels of memories opened and healing began at a cellular level. I realized that, although Pele had catalyzed a great change, the process of unraveling would continue at its own time and in its own way. Patience was one of the lessons my mother's lineage was teaching me.

I found myself reflecting that as I was in Hawaii, I was meeting the ancestors of that place. Why had I not met my ancestors in Canada? Is it easier for us to meet our ancestors when we are not on our home turf? I don't think so. Perhaps, I would not have believed my experiences in my own environment. However, as Hawaii is so spiritual and pure and its link to ancestors so strong, I believe it was easier for me to listen to the ancestors there. Everyone has ancestors. If we believe in them, I am certain they speak to us wherever we are. Still, are we listening? Because I was on vacation rather than working on other projects, I think I was more available than I might have been another time.

Pele waited for her intervention to anchor in me and, grounding in my physical body, I discovered I still stood by the steam vents. I was moved to ask an even more personal question…one, which on some level, I already knew the answer.

"Have ancestors in my two lineages—the moʻo and yours—been enemies in the past?"

"They have, and this is not only your personal story," she answered. "The lunar and solar energies, yin and yang, inner and outer worlds have been in conflict for a thousand years or more. And the ancestors are calling on you to repair this. Do not despair, you are mending strands and it will continue. Always know that what you heal in yourself, you heal in the collective unconscious of humanity. All is woven together."

"But my mother and father had a wonderful marriage and did not fight," I still was not accepting her interpretation wholeheartedly.

"That is true only because your mother assumed the subservient role. If she had been fully in her power, they would have fought. This was partially because of the age in which she was raised and because your father was the head of a household in which she was a servant in a previous life. Because they deeply loved each other, they came into this incarnation to heal the ancestral patterns. You are to continue their work, with the difference that you are to fully own the mo'o power, as well as mine."

Uncomfortable with the responsibility of this revelation, I cast my eyes around for an ally in my leprechaun friend. Pele, sensing my distraction, dismissed me with a slight smile in her voice, "It is enough for now. You will find your Irish friend in the forest. It's too hot for him near me."

Bidding Pele goodbye and, following her guidance, I returned to the visitor's center where Simon had just finished perusing the exhibits. We shared our various experiences and he was as keen as me to follow Pele's directions, so we drove to an older, forested section of the park where she had erupted hundreds of years earlier. What a contrast with Pele's steam vents. Ambling along a trail, we encountered moss-covered rocks and lichen-clad trees housing songbirds singing their little heads off. The cool embrace of the trees encouraged me to take strong breaths to cleanse my lungs of the noxious vapors I'd inhaled at Pele's summit. The misty air allowed her words to settle quietly in the unknown places she had awakened in me. Coming around a bend in the path, I found Lloyd seated beside a large tree. Simon happily continued along the trail giving me time to check in with my Irish friend who he calls Leppie.

"So you found a setting more conducive to your Irish blood," I teased in an attempt to lighten up Pele's disclosure.

"Absolutely. You won't catch me near that sulfur smell and heat. Not at all healthy."

"I would have thought you wanted to meet Pele?"

"Kauai's more to my taste. Water, water, water is what I need. I find the Big Island hard to take with all this fire. Doesn't fit with me frequency. That's why I'm down here where it's nice and cool and, from here, I can meet Pele just fine. Anyway, she needed to see you, not me."

By his unusual subtlety, it was clear that Lloyd knew exactly what had transpired with Pele and its momentous impact on me.

"My moʻokane and menehune teachers have affected me too," he confided, before adding, "And the ancestors."

"What kinds of ancestors are working with you?" I asked, curious to know more about his experiences.

"Many kinds. I've worked for decades with the elemental ancestors we call the old ones. There are human ancestors who come into our realm as well. You're one of those, even though you're in a physical body right now, and there are others not in physical form."

We were only getting started in our conversation, when a group of strange mo'okane manifested in our midst. Lloyd jumped to his feet to show respect and, for once, seemed to have been caught unawares.

"We did not inform your leprechaun friend we were coming, so he wasn't expecting us," an older male addressed me directly.

He didn't resemble any mo'okane that I'd met on Kauai. Although he had a similar body to those mo'okane, he appeared more amorphous, not as solid. He almost blended in with the hazy mist that accompanied them. At the same time, his color inside the mist had a definite red glow to it.

"You look surprised to see mo'o on Pele's slopes. We live everywhere, not just on Kauai, and our tribe is especially adapted to life here. We are very happy to greet both of you and we have come to tell you about our function. We create the mist that accompanies Pele's fire. Those of us, who are dedicated to this, descend into her craters and mix the lava with the air to create mist. The mist brings moisture to this entire area to grow healthy trees and flowers and, after a while, it creates more rain. We do this work in harmony with our brother and sister fire elementals."

"You call yourself mo'o. Yet you more closely resemble mo'okane. Which one are you?" I asked wanting some clarity.

"We are both and neither," he replied, as clear as mud.

Sensing my confusion, the elder explained. "To understand us, you need to learn the lesson we have taught Hawaiians, which is that everything in nature is alive, regardless of the form it has chosen. For example, the old tree that your leprechaun friend sat under is a sentient being in tree form. Hawaiians, unlike haole, do not need to see the tree with a human face to know it is conscious. Still, the stronger the being, the more it can manifest in various bodies. So some spirits, such as the moʻo, or Pele, can take human form. Whether you call us moʻo, or moʻokane, we are all aspects of moʻo and all ancestors. These distinctions only matter to humans in the physical realm. In the astral realm we inhabit, we change shape as we wish and humans who are conscious in the astral realms can do this, too. For example, when they die, most humans choose to create younger bodies than the age they were when they died. I hope you appreciate the difference now that we explained it."

"I understand most of what you're saying, but this idea of ancestors is still evolving in me and it can confuse a non-Hawaiian," I replied, as honestly as I could.

"Most Indigenous people believe in ancestors, it's only you haole who have forgotten us. Ancestors, like Pele and moʻo, are like what you refer to as 'saints' and Hawaiians pray to us and know that we hear their prayers and intercede for them to Spirit.

"Some of us moʻo are known historically, such as our famous moʻo goddess, Kihawahine," the moʻo answered proudly. "She married a Hawaiian chief and this lineage has interbred in the Hawaiian royalty since that time. Kihawahine's influence was so important that King Kamehameha the Great married a ten-year-old princess called Keopuolani to inherit the girl's sacred lineage and then conquered the islands in Kihawahine's name. Even today, the Dragon Clan on Molokai trace their lineage back to her, so her influence is not past."

I was congratulating myself on understanding his last points, when he introduced a completely foreign idea to my western mind. "Another thing," he said. "Humans who have strong mana, what you think of as spiritual power, can become not only an ancestor, but THIS ancestor."

"How exactly would that work?" I was left in the dark…again.

"If you come from a western tradition, you might say that Mother Mary IS the Divine Mother—the great Cosmic being who creates all form in our universe. Or as a Hindu, you might think the goddess Kali IS the Divine Mother," he replied with exaggerated patience.

"I think I get it. It's similar to when Jesus, speaking of his relationship with God, the ultimate ancestor, said, 'My Father and I are one'. This means that as we evolve spiritually, our personality unites more and more with the great spiritual beings (godlike ancestors) who oversee our evolution. So Jesus can be a Christ and Krishna can be a Christ and ultimately you and I, if all goes well, can be too."

"Yes, that's the idea," the mo'o responded. "In our Hawaiian tradition, Kaili'ohe Kame'ekua, who told the *Tales of the Night Rainbow*—which is the best source of mo'o myths—actually became the mo'o ancestor Kihawahine."

"I appreciate you taking the time to explain this. I now understand in theory, if not fully in practice, who the ancestors are and how important they are to everyone. I feel that the ancestors are still reawakening parts of me to really KNOW and LIVE the reality that you are expressing. And I have another question that I forgot to ask Pele."

Hearing this, Lloyd rolled his eyes. Not deterred, I continued. "Stories about Pele relate that she was an enemy of the mo'o and that she killed them, however in the old traditions, the king of the mo'o was her uncle."

"When Hawaiians use the words aunt or uncle, it's a term of respect for their elders," the mo'o explained. "This older story indicates that the mo'o were here before Pele and that she respected them. Although we live on the earth that Pele created, before earth, there was water, so moʻo were here before her.

"Because we're located on a South Pacific Island where water is the dominant element, moʻo ancestors choose to rule the element of water, rather than fire or air, like other dragons. Yet, we moʻo on the Big Island work with the fire part of our nature. Because your past life lineage is traced back through the kāhuna to moʻo and the aliʻi to Pele, both of us have chosen you to share our story."

With those last words, he and the entire group of ancestors vanished. Absorbed by the conversation with the elder, I'd been largely unaware of Lloyd and was amazed that he'd remained quiet.

"When a group of ancestors chooses to speak to you, I am quiet. Why did you think I got to me feet so quickly? But now that you ask (I was not asking) I have something to share that would interest you. Did you know that the word moʻo means a lineage and a spine?"

"I'm intrigued. Say more."

"Have you heard the Hawaiians say that they like to 'talk story?' Telling their story is very important to them and a story in Hawaiian is called *moʻolelo*, which is a progression of words strung along the spine of the moʻo. You are getting to know how important lineage is to Hawaiians. Well, the very word genealogy, or *moʻokuʻauhau*, describes the interlocking bones of the spine of a moʻo."

Beaming with pride that he could share his new knowledge with the human, he departed. Although new information continued to come through my conversations with Pele and the moʻo, I felt I could see the outline of the puzzle that had been given to me to assemble. Fortunately, I was soon to meet a teacher who could shed light on some remaining dark areas.

Serge Kahili King, Huna Teacher

I first met Serge Kahili King in 1986. Neither of us can remember how we were introduced, but we both knew Sun Bear, who was leading a Native American ceremony on the Big Island where I was teaching, so that is a possibility. Serge's books and teaching on Hawaiian huna are internationally recognized and I was looking forward to seeing him again.

Serge has been a student of Hawaiian culture and spiritual wisdom since the age of 14 when his father began teaching him. A Hawaiian man, Joseph Kahili, adopted Serge's father and trained him in this knowledge. Interestingly, Serge's father chose to teach Serge, but not his siblings, to develop huna powers. He was taught how to communicate with plants and animals and to do mental chess and play other games.

At his father's death, Serge at age 17 left the spiritual path for a short time and moved to California. He became disenchanted living without deeper meaning in his life and, when he re-met the Kahili family, he re-committed to huna studies. Joseph adopted Serge as his grandson and turned Serge's training over to his son and daughter.

Because each Hawaiian family has their own ancestors and spiritual teachings, his teachings are grounded in the Kahili tradition and the ancestral guardians are the dolphin and owl.

Near the end of my time on the Big Island, Simon and I went to see Serge hoping to speak with him about the information I was receiving. I wanted to check my experiences with a well-respected teacher of huna. We were catching up on 30 years of living, when I realized that I'd better record the pearls of huna that Serge was sharing.

"Let's talk about the menehune for a moment," said Serge. "The word menehune has a double meaning and the equivalent word in Tahitian is *manahune*. It means 'people of the secret power' because mana means 'power'. The word was used by the Tahitians also to mean 'people of little power', or commoners, because *hune* means 'something small' and also poor. Huna can also mean something very indefinite, like mist, which is difficult to see. This last definition for huna refers to esoteric knowledge, which the menehune were known to have.

"The oldest chants state that when the Polynesians first came to Hawaii there were three races. The first race was the *nawa* meaning 'the noisy ones' and stories about menehune speak of how they were noisy. For example, when they finished building a temple at the top of Kokee on Kauai, the shouting was so loud it scared the birds on Oahu. Menehune were also called 'the banana eaters', as that was their primary carbohydrate source. They might have been smaller as they were not eating meat, but nothing in the ancient chants said they were.

"The second race was the *nawao* and *wao* is the term for 'wilderness' and the second race were giants who were always found in the wilderness. The third race was the *namu* and the word means 'the silent ones'. The namu were the ones who carried the esoteric knowledge and used telepathy. When the Polynesians came, there are many tales about how they drove all three menehune peoples into the hills and remote areas. Later, when westerners came to Hawaii, they could not comprehend these stories. So they changed the Hawaiian story to the little people story of menehune being something like leprechauns.

"Even today there are people who say their ancestors are menehune in the sense we have been talking about. Some of these ancestors were small people and some giants. Hawaiians are not a homogenous people. There are many races that have come here with various traditions at different times, so they have a hard time agreeing on anything. They are not clans or tribes. They are family groups which can lead to problems in this political world."

Serge's account complemented the one I heard from Barry Brailsford, a cultural anthropologist, who wrote about the Waitaha of New Zealand. I said to Serge, "According to the Waitaha, they were the original people of New Zealand and, when the Maori came, the Waitaha went underground to avoid being persecuted and killed. They kept their traditions secret for 700 years and only in the last few decades have they asked Barry to tell their story. The Waitaha, like the menehune, are three races. A Polynesian race, a yellow-skinned, slanted-eye race, and the ones they call the fairy people who had reddish hair, freckles, and fair skin."

"Speaking of red hair," said Serge, "in Hawaiian tradition, this feature is called *ehu*. These people were highly regarded as being very special and Kamehameha the Great was said to have reddish hair. The Hawaiians believe either these red-haired people came from the stars, or that they were always in Polynesia. My family taught that, when our people came from the stars, there were already people here."

"This area could include ancient Lemuria, couldn't it?" I asked. "All the Polynesian and pre-Polynesian people could have come from there?"

"Yes, and I use the word Mu," he replied,

"What you have said about the three kinds of menehune is very helpful as it tallies with the different kinds I met. Could you tell me what you know about the moʻo?"

"No one has done anything in-depth on the moʻo. The word means 'lizard' but it was a family group of people, too. In Hawaii, each family specializes in a certain skill and on Easter Island, the moʻo people were the ones who created the large head sculptures. They were well known in ancient Hawaii as being magicians and sorcerers, but remember that missionaries called everything sorcery that was spiritual and outside of Christianity. Pele legends are full of conflict between the Pele and Moʻo families, because the Pele people also had magic and sorcery."

I was astounded to hear that Pele had similar spiritual gifts as the moʻo. This meant I received my spiritual gifts not only from my mother, but also from my father's lineage. A double whammy. Pele obviously wanted me to hear the news from someone other than her. In other words a human, like Serge, whose authority I would trust.

Serge continued, "In the older legends, there is no mention of Pele and in Pele legends, there are no stories about most of the menehune or other gods, except for Lono, the god of rain and fertility. He was her uncle in the story, which indicates that he preceded her. As a result, we know that Pele is not as old as the moʻo.

"Pele came originally from Kahiki which means literally 'out of sight', 'beyond the horizon'. The Hawaiian word for Tahiti is also *kahiki* and in Tahitian, the word kahiki means 'to transform'. In the Hawaiian language, there are five kahikis—ascending levels from the horizon (kahiki) until you are in outer space. So when you hear the word 'kahiki' in the legends, it could mean outer space or another island system. There is no way to tell, but gods and goddesses usually come from kahiki. Kauai sometimes was called kahiki because it was the most spiritual island and also because it was the farthest away from the Big Island."

"One of the things I find most difficult to understand is that Hawaiian words have so many diverse meanings," I shared with Serge. "You can't pin anything down, words move in another direction when you try."

Serge smiled in understanding at what I was saying.

"Hawaiians do not think chronologically and did not keep track of dates," he said. "There was no date known until 1778 when Cook arrived. Hawaiians recorded their genealogy in their chants. The purpose in Hawaiian was not to have a historical record, but to demonstrate the present lineage, which is vertical—not horizontal—as in the west. In the Hawaiian language, there is no past or future tense. Everything is related to the present moment. For example, when Hawaiians speak of the past they say, 'As of this moment, my going to Kona last week is over'. This means in the Hawaiian way of speaking that past events only exist in relation to the present moment."

"The reality that the ancestors are eternally present has been growing in me over these last years," I began. "It's very different from western thinking of ancestors only in the past, which minimalizes their impact on our lives. Seeing the ancestors in the present, which is how most Indigenous cultures see them, increases their importance in our lives and makes us accountable to them."

Because Serge is a psychologist, I knew he would follow my next points. "I've been thinking about how the ancestors can re-emerge for westerners and see this idea dovetailing with my work on the body elemental and the unconscious. Our body elemental (you could call it the consciousness of the etheric body) builds our body in each lifetime, and puts in information from our physical, astral, causal, and spiritual experiences from other lives. Through psychotherapy and dream work, for example, we can access these patterns to heal past and present life trauma and release our authentic selves to access our strengths and achieve our life purpose. I think the body elemental, which for most people is largely unconscious, lives in the eternal present and is in touch with our ancestors."

Serge listened attentively to see where I was taking this idea.

"Because Hawaiians inherit their stories orally and only from their specific family," I continued, "if parents don't repeat the stories to their children, the family not only forgets the stories, but loses the connection with their ancestors and cannot turn to them for help. The stories are a bridge between the physical and astral world, and if the people don't know the stories of their lineage the connection is broken."

Saddened by the even broader implication for non-Hawaiians, I elaborated. "In western culture, we've lost our connection to our ancestors because we don't know the stories."

Serge was so helpful in his discussion about ancestors that I thought he might know something about elementals. I asked. "Is there any mention of elementals in the Hawaiian tradition? For example, in England there are brownies, in Germany, elves."

"Yes, we have that. We have the *peke* and *e'paa*, which are different kinds of spirits with diverse characteristics. *Kino* Lau means 'many bodies' and all strong spirits and gods have many bodies. For example, Pele was the spirit in the molten lava and her various forms were those of an old, mature, or young woman, but she could appear as a white dog, fire, lava, wind, clouds, thunder, and lightning. She was also associated with the 'ohelo plant that grows on the slopes of the volcanoes. In Hawaiian tradition, there is no supernatural; there is visible and invisible, but all is nature. In Hawaiian, we don't see a fire elemental as a flame so much as one of the forms of the goddess Pele. One of her lovers was a Pan-like god of the wilderness."

As an aside, Serge added, "The Kahili family did not worship any of the goddesses, but called upon them as friends to evoke certain qualities, aspects, or powers of healing."

"In one of my books, *Hybrids*, I speak of 22 different ancestors that humans might have descended from, such as elementals, dolphins, angels, giants, and dragons. There is even a Pan hybrid who is the god of the wilderness and the ancestor of elementals. These ancestors are the same as Hawaiians saying they were descended from menehune or mo'o."

"This is very interesting," interjected Serge, "and in Hawaii, you have a lot of shark people, too."

"Oops. I didn't include shark people," I replied.

"There's something interesting about the shark people. I wrote an article called *Dolphin Stories of Hawaii* and yet, even in the oldest books of legends, there are no dolphin stories. This puzzled me because dolphins are part of my family heritage. Then I was reading South Pacific legends and in one, there was a goddess named Ena who called two sharks to give her a ride on their backs to another island. They weren't going fast enough, so she hit them on their forehead. And in the legend it said, 'Even today all sharks have bumps on their forehead'. In reality, sharks don't have bumps on their foreheads, but dolphins do. And sharks don't give rides to people, dolphins do.

"The problem occurred with the translators. The word used for shark in Hawaiian was *mano*, but this was a generic word for animals that have teeth, swim in the surf, have a high dorsal fin, and give live birth: in other words, dolphins and sharks. You have all this dolphin behavior in the shark tales, such as rescuing people who fall in the water, and coming up to be petted by people in boats, and becoming friends with people. Obviously the translators got it wrong."

I was happy to hear that I had not missed a hybrid and that there really was a dolphin ancestor. At that point, our conversation came to a natural conclusion as our stomachs were urging us to have lunch. Serge and the ancestors had answered most of my questions and I needed time for the seeds planted in Hawaii to come to fruition.

Lessons from Hawaii

The process of integration that began in Hawaii continued over the next months in Canada. I felt pieces of the puzzle shift into place, but on a level that I couldn't put into words. The most pressing questions I had concerned the ancestors. Who were they—in all their aspects—and what was their role in the lives not only of Hawaiians, but of all humans? A friend of mine is a Jungian psychologist and speaking with her was especially helpful in pulling my insights to the surface.

"Because the doors to other realms have always been open for you," Honor said, "you have not found just one system, such as elementals or hybrids, and said, 'That's it!' These names are just a manifestation of what you are seeing when you have these amazing astral experiences.

"One of the problems with humans is that we want to concretize. We need to realize that beings are manifestations of an energy, a beingness rather than a thingness. Whatever particular cultural traditions we belong to, we seek to clothe this energy with the images from that culture, but that gets static. We have to break down the icons and smash the statues over and over again to stay in touch with what is occurring on an experiential level of the astral or spiritual."

"I have been wondering how to express who ancestors are and their importance to us today," I said.

"Even bringing that idea into your diverse strands might be helpful for people. It really doesn't matter how individuals internalize it or bring it into their life, whether they think an ancestor is an actual being like Mother Mary who lived, or that they recognize that Mother Mary is an expression of an archetype that is an experience of Divine connection.

"On the deepest sub-atomic level, it is just energy," Honor said. "Carl Jung had an interesting concept where he talked about how one end of the archetype is matter and the other end is Spirit and they may be manifestations of the same thing. Humans need to grab things and hold on to them and have a sensual experience of an image."

I found Honor's ideas helpful. "I agree with you. I feel my work with elementals, hybrids, and now ancestors are opening doors to the astral world. But it's still only pieces, not the whole."

"These are strands of the mystery," said Honor. "We can't begin to encompass the entire mystery of what the Divine is. So we grab little strands and give them names and form in order to understand a piece because we live in form, in matter."

"It's like an onion," I replied, "where we peel back more and more layers of understanding throughout our life. When we first get these glimpses, it's difficult to understand mentally. We feel we have crossed to a new land. But it's hard to know what that new land is, because we see it through the mist. There is no going back to the old land and it will take a while, whether that is weeks, or years, or a lifetime to know the new reality."

My conversation with Honor helped me to let go of the need to define my experiences. I committed to writing what had transpired, as the ancestors and others had requested, and trusted them with the process. My leprechaun friend was conspicuously absent during this time and not even cups of tea drew him. Finally, one rainy Sunday morning, he appeared in his favorite chair, looking out the window at the ocean. He no longer wore his Hawaiian clothes, but was bundled up for a Canadian early spring.

"Miss me?" he smirked, reaching for the tea.

"I know you're busy trying to get the menehune and moʻokane settled with human partners, so I'm patient," I replied.

"Much appreciated. But I'm here now to shed light on any remaining questions you have."

"It's not so much questions at this stage. It's more that I want to run my ideas by you to see if they tally with what you know."

"Go on."

"Initially, I tried to put my encounters with the menehune, moʻokane, and ancestors through filters of what I had known before, but they didn't fit. This caused me to remove those filters, one by one. Oh sure, I probably still have filters, but now they are full of holes."

The leprechaun remained perfectly still, giving no clue if I was on the right track. Not to be put off, I said, "Let's start with the menehune. The first time I met menehune I thought they were elementals and this is what the majority of Hawaiians think, too. Then they told me that they were the original inhabitants of Hawaii and that some humans, even in the present day, claim to be descended from them. At this moment, I realize that there is truth in both of these observations, but the menehune cannot be defined exclusively by either definition. It is nebulous, if I try to come up with one right answer. I've come to accept that they are their own kind of being and do not need to be grouped with any other race."

"And what about the moʻokane?" he asked in a neutral tone.

"It's the same thing. Originally, I thought the moʻokane were elementals, but something about them didn't fit this definition. It was as if they had greater depth. Don't get me wrong, Lloyd, I don't mean an insult. What I'm trying to say is that they had a stronger ego, more like you. Then, when I heard they were descended from the moʻo, I tried to fit them into that slot as dragon hybrids with human characteristics. This worked for a while, until I started to wonder if moʻokane were ancestors as well. I was not able to categorize them."

"Speaking of the moʻo…" Lloyd prodded me to continue.

"When Serge explained that Pele could choose a multitude of forms, my last vestiges of wanting to confine the moʻo to only one physical form dissolved. I then got it, right down to the cells of my body, that the moʻo weren't only water dragons, but could also be the rainbow deva in the waterfall, and the being of the mist who spoke to me at the top of Kokee. Daisy told me not to focus on defining the beings, but to realize that the teachings, no matter who was speaking, were the important thing."

"This brings us to the ancestors." Lloyd crossed his legs nonchalantly and, raising the cup to his mouth, took a big slurp.

"Reconnecting with the ancestors has been the most precious experience of all. But it wasn't easy. Spirit plopped me right in the middle of a strange land and said, 'Figure it out.'"

"And what did you learn?"

"At first, I thought ancestors were both dead ali'i royalty and kāhuna shaman in the Spirit realm who were guarding the sacred heiau (temples) from trespassers and trying to keep that knowledge pure for their Hawaiian descendants. I didn't know how—or if—this related to me. Then, I was told repeatedly that I'd had Hawaiian lives, both as a kahuna and ali'i. A still greater stretch was to learn of my mo'o lineage, and, it was even more unsettling when Pele informed me that she was my ancestor as well. It's been a long haul figuring out why Spirit took me on this journey of discovery and what these revelations mean, for me, and for others."

"And…" His right hand took a firmer hold on the cup, and his left hand waved impatient circles.

Trying to hurry up, I got out, "Before my experiences in Hawaii, I hadn't grasped that ancestors are continually present helping and guiding everyone's life."

"For example…?" Lloyd interjected, now wanting more.

"I now appreciate the various kinds of ancestors that each of us have," I continued. "For example, we have physical ancestors, such as Grandma and Grandpa. That's easy. We also have human ancestors from our past lives. These people helped us then and because there is no time or space in higher realms where ancestors dwell, many of these people still help us in the present. We also have a hybrid lineage, our original lineage, from when we started incarnating on Earth. This could be as a dolphin, mo'o, angel, elemental, or many other kinds of beings. In addition, we also have the great spiritual teachers we've committed to in the past, like Krishna, Jesus, Tara, and Buffalo Calf Woman."

"And why is having ancestors important?" Patience not being one of his virtues, Lloyd was becoming increasingly assertive.

"These various kinds of ancestors in the astral realm are always connected to us. Depending on their frequencies, which stem from the diverse realms they inhabit in the astral world, they influence us in various ways."

The leprechaun sat waiting for me to proceed.

"Let's look at it this way. Humans are conscious in the physical realm, but there is an astral and even higher causal (pure thought) realm where most humans are unconscious. The menehune and elementals have all these realms, too, but theirs are on different frequencies than ours. The more frequencies that humans or elementals or ancestors are conscious in, the more realms they can access and the more beings they can communicate with. Consciousness exists in many ways in many realms and humans, even you, my friend, only see a small part of this. The good news is that nothing really dies, not ancestors, not you, not me."

The leprechaun exhaled his breath in relief. "You might have thought that I was withholding information, but I've been a student along with you. I, too, was in a foreign land finding my way in Hawaii. I can easily travel to the realms of the menehune and mo'okane because their frequencies are closer to the human realms where I'm proficient. But it's quite another matter for me to talk with many of the spiritual ancestors. Their realms are in a higher frequency than I can visit on my own. You are a bridge for me to go there."

"Ahh. So the human has been of use," I sent an image of him riding piggyback on me.

His seriousness dissolved and he bent over laughing.

"Kidding aside," I said, "Now that I'm beginning to understand how many ancestors are helping me, I feel humbled and grateful at the same time. I continually receive information to go forward and have confidence in the clarity of my vision. Lately, the most meaningful confirmation of all occurred and it concerns you."

"Well, if it concerns me, I'm all ears," he said, sending me an image of himself covered in ears.

"About the same time I met you over 20 years ago, I started reading books by an Indian yogi, Paramahansa Yogananda. His bridging of the western and eastern paths fits me and one of the things he writes about is the Christ. The east, unlike the west, stresses one's spiritual lineage and Yogananda's master was Sri Yukteswar who, I must admit, I feel even closer to. He is stern, but his great gift is wisdom, which I resonate with."

"And how does this concern me?" asked the leprechaun, gazing at his cuticles.

"I'm getting to that. I was re-reading Yogananda's book *Autobiography of a Yogi* and came to a section that impacted me greatly. Sri Yukteswar manifested in a physical body after death to give his disciple a message. He told Yogananda that he was working in the astral world where 'fairies, mermaids, fishes, animals, goblins, gnomes, demigods and spirits all reside in different astral planets'.

"All of a sudden I realized, not just mentally, but with deep knowing, that Sri Yukteswar was, and is, my spiritual ancestor. Not only mine, of course, thousands of people would say the same, but that does not lessen his importance in my life. And I hope you're listening to this part: He brought me to Ireland to write about elementals like goblins and gnomes, which is where you come in, Lloyd. But it doesn't end there. I believe he gave me the idea to research and then write about hybrids like the mermaids he speaks of. And you were involved with that, too. And now I see him guiding me to write about ancestors, which he refers to as 'demigods'. There are so many synchronicities that I know Sri Yukteswar is directing my destiny and that my life is in service to a much greater plan. One that is largely unknown by me and which is revealed on a need-to-know basis when the time is right."

A smile began to form at the corners of Lloyd's mouth as my revelation drew to a close. "So," I asked, "do you see that we've been brought together to do our work?"

"One problem… he hasn't mentioned leprechauns. Just a slight oversight, one I'm sure can be corrected," he guffawed, downing the last of his tea.

PART 2:

How Ancestors Influence Us Today

Thank you for taking the time to journey with me. My story may have triggered ways in which ancestors have already contacted you. If so, I am pleased for you. Perhaps, on the other hand, this is the first time you have considered the importance of either physical/biological or spiritual ancestors. In any event, if you are now drawn to seek out your ancestors, I'd like to offer some ideas as to how and where to start.

For me, the most important revelation was that we have many kinds of biological and spiritual ancestors and that some of these are affecting us now. When most of us think of ancestors, we think of blood ancestors who have lived in the past and from whom we have received DNA and learned family patterns. Examining our blood lineage is important as the increasing popularity of websites like Ancestry.com, FamilySearch.org and WikiTree.com attests. Our motivation for engaging in these practices might stem from curiosity to discover where we come from and the gifts of our lineage to healing ourselves and not passing our family wounds onto our descendants.

Thinking of ancestors in a linear way, which is how most often we view our physical ancestors ranging from past to the present (great-grandmother > grandmother > mother > daughter) does not accurately represent the multi-dimensional reality in which our ancestors exist. Rather than viewing ancestors as existing only in the past, it is essential to embrace the reality that they exist, like us, in all dimensions, including those outside of space and time. Yet, they can influence us from these non-physical realms.

It may be difficult to embrace this idea that, although we can't see something like the ancestors, they influence our lives. We think we are conscious, but we aren't. For example, look at your body. You only see the front of your body and have no idea what the back looks like. Yet, the unseen back half is there, containing the being you think of as you. Just as you cannot live without the back half of your body, you cannot live without the multi-dimensional astral and causal worlds from which come your feelings and thoughts manifesting as your physical reality. These astral and causal realms are where the ancestors dwell.

Ancestors in physical lineage include our family (such as parents/ grandparents/ etc.), our tribe (Celtic/Jewish/Sioux/etc.), and our nation (Canadian/ German/ Egyptian/ etc.). For instance, if our ancestors descend from Ireland (even if we were not born in Ireland) we carry within our genes the poverty and suffering of the Irish people who endured successive famines. And if we have

German heritage, we inherit the trauma of two world wars. For this reason, many individuals with German heritage feel guilty for something that happened long before their birth.

Let me go further. The land on which we dwell carries a memory of what has happened on that land and these themes transfer to the people who live there presently. For example, if our country was occupied by enemy forces during war, we might become suspicious of others and have scarcity mentality. We might worry about where our next meal is coming from—even though this attitude has no relevance to our present life which is actually abundant.

It is important that we don't immerse ourselves in blame or self-flagellation due to actions of our physical, tribal or national ancestors. ALL of us have been both victims and persecutors in our past lives, and perhaps even in our present life, but blaming self or others will never take us out of the cycle of wounding. Only compassion and forgiveness will do this. In fact, because of both our victim and persecutor human heritage, it is more common that we may find ourselves a blend of both guilt and self-righteousness, fear and arrogance.

Actually, if we are fully to include ALL of our physical, biological ancestors, we need to acknowledge that our biological heritage ultimately includes all beings (animals/plants/birds/etc.) on this planet because we all evolved from the same chemical stew billions of years ago. This is the foundation and life view that Indigenous peoples around the world have always maintained and, as science is continually reinforcing this truth now, this understanding is moving into our mainstream consciousness.

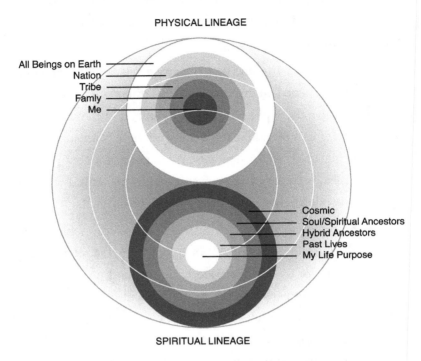

PHYSICAL LINEAGE

All Beings on Earth
Nation
Tribe
Family
Me

Cosmic
Soul/Spiritual Ancestors
Hybrid Ancestors
Past Lives
My Life Purpose

SPIRITUAL LINEAGE

Physical and Spiritual Lineages connect and interpenetrate each other

Our spiritual lineage, because it is non-visible, is not as obvious as our physical/biological lineage, but is equally as important. To believe in spiritual ancestors we need to realize that other realities exist where elementals, angels, and many mythical beings, such as dragons, dwell. Whether we are aware of this or not, these beings also influence and guide our lives.

These astral realms where ancestors dwell exist outside of space and time and we have now entered the era in human evolution when we will begin to access these realms consciously. The astral worlds of elementals and ancestors interpenetrate the third-dimensional reality of our visible world and it is our destiny to become conscious in these invisible realms.

To understand the many kinds of spiritual ancestors in these unseen realms, it may help to refer to the diagram on page 146. The first rung on the spiritual lineage ladder, and the one that most people may be familiar with, is their past lives. Our past lives include the diverse countries in which we have lived, and the variety of racial and religious traditions we have experienced. It has been my experience, and that of many people that I have led on past life regressions, that most often we are our own ancestors from our past lives. This means, if you see yourself having a past life starving in Ireland, you may have passed down this wound genetically through successive generations to yourself in the present day where, bringing it to consciousness, you can heal it right back in time to that original starving life.

The second rung is our "hybrid" lineage, which is the race from which we originated. For example, although we have a human body this lifetime, we may be descended from an angel, elemental, dolphin, or dragon. In other words, we may not only be an Earth being but also an Interstellar being. Interstellar beings are mentioned in human myths around the world and have been seen across the ages by seers in all spiritual traditions. They exist in astral and causal realms—the realms where ancestors dwell—and these realms are starting to become accessible to us. It is too much to go into this topic in detail at this time however, if you are interested, I encourage you to read more about your hybrid lineage in my book, *Hybrids: So you think you are human.*

Another spiritual lineage of beings who have guided us through many lifetimes, may not obviously have biological links to us, although as I said earlier, ALL beings on higher levels are linked to each other. This higher spiritual lineage works essentially with our soul, unlike our physical/biological ancestors that work predominantly with our personality. These soul/spiritual ancestors would include Saints and Ascended Masters, such as Paramahansa Yogananda, Archangel Michael, Kihawahine the moʻo goddess, and Mother Mary. Saints are old souls and some, like the Dalai Lama, Mother Theresa, and Gandhi, whether physically alive or deceased, guide thousands of people.

Still higher, is our Cosmic spiritual lineage, which you and I have in common with all humanity. Here we find the Cosmic Christ and the Divine Mother who oversee the evolution of all humanity and the evolution of our entire universe.

There may also be ancestors who share both our physical/biological and spiritual lineage. These ancestors may well be alive today and when we meet them, we recognize them from past lives. We often reincarnate in soul groups. For example, when we hear someone speak of a young child and say, 'She reminds me of my grandmother', that child may be a reincarnation of the grandmother who died, became an ancestor, and now is back in body again. The more we become aware of both our biological and spiritual ancestors, the more we see and feel their influence upon us and how our individual lives intertwine with all beings, human and otherwise, on Earth and in the Cosmos.

Ancestors make themselves known to us if we are willing to listen—especially when we have something unresolved or wounded in our family, tribe, or national lineage. The ancestors are here to help us. They support us in healing emotional wounds, such as abuse, abandonment, lack of love and addictions in our family line. Simultaneously, they reveal the gifts and strengths handed down to us in these same lines—gifts that empower us to fulfill our purpose. They also steer us in a direction they wish us to go, so when doors to our desired goals open and close for no logical reason, we might look for their influence in our lives.

They often lead us in small, subtle ways, such as becoming aware of synchronicities. For example, my stepdaughter and my mother have the same birthday, and my other stepdaughter, who was adopted from Columbia, shares the same birthday as her adoptive father.

Another way ancestors nudge us is through recurring patterns. Do we marry…sometimes more than once…a person like our mother or father? Do we remeet people later in life that we have known earlier? Do we fail whenever we do a particular task and always succeed whenever we do another task? If we pay attention to these "coincidences", they may reveal ancestral patterns we need to explore.

As well as our physical lineage, we might have a wounding in our spiritual lineage. This is our past lives, hybrid, or soul/spiritual lineage. Our wounding or unresolved issue often exists on more than one of these levels. For example, an issue we have identified in our life might be the same one our mother has and we both could have shared this same issue in a past life.

Furthermore, we could have a negative pattern handed down in our family line, (i.e. alcoholism, suicide, desertion of a parent) and it may be a spiritual ancestor, one *not* in our blood lineage who will help us heal our wound. Why? Because until we do, we must reincarnate again and again to face this same issue thereby delaying our spiritual progress, which is something that our spiritual ancestor is attempting to prevent.

Ancestors come from all countries and dwell in a great diversity of realms in the astral world. There is no limit to the number of ancestors we might have, but not all of them have a message for us. The ancestors who approach us do so because they wish us to act in some way; perhaps repair a wounding in one of our lineages or use our gifts/skills to fulfill a task they give us. But this is not a one-way relationship. They support us in fulfilling our purpose in this life and are strengthened and happy when we do so. Because they can see more of our soul's purpose and gifts, they know what we are capable of, sometimes better than we do. They know that if we heal a trauma or weakness in our personality, we will become the person that we can be, not only in this life, but in all our lives.

Ancestral memories reveal themselves when something in our inner or outer life triggers them. This could be a physical problem that cannot be cured by doctors or psychological pain that cannot be cured by therapy. Pieces of the puzzle line up and we will begin to see a pattern emerging. But all is not revealed at once. A complex puzzle requires our willing participation to bring the complete picture into focus. This is how the unconscious becomes known. As we participate in the journey, more light is shed on the pieces until we see the whole picture.

We are at the beginning of the new science of epigenetics, which suggests that not only the physical but also the psychological wounds we have suffered alter our genes. These wounds leave molecular scars as memories that adhere to our DNA and get transferred to our descendants. Epigenetics lends credence to how alcoholism, sexual abuse, even genocide of our Indigenous peoples gets passed down. But hold on: We also inherit positive, emotional experiences in the same way, so if we have received love and support from our family, this gets passed along with other gifts and talents we may have inherited from our physical ancestors, such as talents in music or mathematics, having a strong and healthy body, etc. And the more we honor these gifts, the more fully they are activated for use in our present life. All ancestor's gifts are available to us NOW.

Let's take a look at the importance of this quest. If we heal our ancestral wounds, even at the family level, this positively impacts all levels of the wounding, which can occur at the cultural, religious, or national level. As an example, many children of parents who went through wars, or children of Indigenous peoples who were taken from their families and sent to residential school, have the same patterns of fear and wounding as their parents and grandparents. If the child can heal the wound, it rewinds through space and time to heal the ancestral wound. If we have difficulty believing this, it helps to remember that time, as we know it, does not exist. In the astral world where the ancestors reside (where we go in dreams and in between lives) past and future exist in the present. Again, this means when we heal our wounds, we heal these patterns not only for our descendants, but also for our ancestors. It is our responsibility and privilege to do this for our descendants, our ancestors, and ourselves.

Often ancestors will not leave us in peace until we heal the wound and this process can be painful. Guilt, fear, and psychosomatic illnesses may be symptoms of our unconscious unwillingness to examine what they want us to understand. I don't want to create the idea that ancestors are tyrants. Instead, think of them as they were when they were physically alive. We might observe that there is a great difference between the consciousness of our deceased father, for example, with that of the Christ. Perhaps our father wants us to cure a wound that he created and then passed to his descendants. If so, don't wait for Christ... start working with your deceased father right now. From his vantage point in the astral world, he is very aware of any damage he may have done, but the wounding can best be healed by someone currently embodied.

Of course, we always have free will to do this or not. But when we heal a wound in our family, whether through family constellation therapy, shamanistic practices, spiritual transformation, or by other means, the effects are much greater than we imagine as it contributes to the healing of our tribe and nation. Just as our physical ancestors give us our physical inheritance, our spiritual ancestors work with our soul to assist us in fulfilling our purpose, not only in this life, but in all lives. As we honor our spiritual ancestors, we reclaim soul fragments from past lives that we can then reintegrate back into the psychic flow that empowers us in our present life.

To fully achieve our purpose, we are called to unlock the doors to all parts of our unconscious and to bring what is unconscious to consciousness. The good news is that each of us has a body elemental within us to help. Our body elemental is Spirit in form. It is the consciousness that builds our physical, emotional, mental, and spiritual body. It builds our body and personality with the strengths and weaknesses we need to achieve our purpose. It draws on both positive and negative patterns—including those of our ancestors—that have been created in previous incarnations. Some of these patterns are conscious, while others are unconscious.

Both our biological and spiritual lineage is encoded in us by our body elemental. Our body elemental can assist us to heal negative ancestral patterns and reinstate positive, life-giving ones. As we heal the patterns of our personal ancestors, ultimately, we will be healing the collective unconscious of humanity that renowned transpersonal psychiatrist Carl Jung says has accumulated over millions of years.

Why? Because war, famine, violence, prejudice, loss, and grief are not new. These problems have existed as long as there have been humans, and they must be transformed into love, peace, wisdom, compassion, gratitude, forgiveness, and joy. This may seem like an overwhelming task, but we are set up to succeed, not fail, and Spirit gives us only the piece to do for which we alone are responsible.

The importance of the ancestors lies not only in the wisdom they offer, but also in the journey necessary to acquire it. It crafts us to make us worthy of receiving their wisdom; conversely, receiving their wisdom increases our worthiness. Ancestors reveal themselves piece by piece, letting us digest each morsel before adding another bit for us to consume. And like any tasty dish, once we start, we want to eat it all. Although we may not always be aware of their work, the ancestors are master strategists for our good in service to creating a conscious world.

Journeying in spiritual realms is not the same as getting in a car and driving from point A to B. It is more like a mystery story where we pick up hints that gradually add up and make sense as we arrive at our destination. The spiritual realms are more of a both/and than an either/or and the more we seek to concretize our experiences, the more these realms elude us. In the astral realms, ancestors (as well as elementals, angels, etc.) can take any shape they wish and they often reveal new aspects of themselves to us when we are ready to know these. This can be uncomfortable for our ego that wants to know "exactly" what these beings are, and travelling without clear directions is challenging. Our ego desires control but, if we honestly examine our life, we realize we cannot control our life in the physical world either and that life in both seen and unseen realms is a great evolving mystery.

Indigenous people are more connected to their ancestors than western Europeans and we can learn from them. In modern western culture, we separate the head (thinking) from the heart (feeling), thereby breaking the vital connection to our body, our ancestors, and the Earth. We have lost the stories of our parents, family, tribe, country, and origins. Many Indigenous cultures, such as those of North and South American, Australia and New Zealand, as well as communities in Tibet, Mongolia, and Africa still have this link. It is the link to BEING and Indigenous peoples keep ancestral links alive by telling stories of their origins and these accounts have the power to transform both listener and speaker because they are heard by both the brain and the heart, and the heart is where real transformation occurs.

The Hawaiian culture is grounded on a belief in ancestors and, like other Indigenous cultures, its people recognize a kinship with all creation. To them, nature and all beings are alive, not only in the physical world, but in all realms and dimensions. Each human being is a part of the whole and affects and is influenced by the great web of life. This is the message from the Hawaiian ancestors; not just in theory, but as a participatory reality for today.

Stories of Indigenous people, such as those of Hawaii, speak about their kinship with all living beings, not only humans, but animals, plants, and the unseen, as well as the seen world. Indigenous peoples talk about their power animals (in Hawaii the aumakua) the animals that speak to them and with whom they are related. When we realize that 98 percent of our genetic code is shared with animals, we are on the way to knowing that this relationship is not a metaphor; it is reality.

Hawaii, and especially Kauai, is special for another reason. Because it is located 3,000 miles from any large land mass, nature is pure and virginal there. When the African elder and shaman Malidoma Some went to Kauai, he wept with joy stating that the vitality was so pure that he could feel it penetrating the collective consciousness of the Earth without distortion and spreading throughout the universe.

We, in the western world, have lost our connection to this web of Being. The word "human" actually comes from the Latin meaning *humus*, the word for soil or earth; yet we are rootless. In our quest to master our environment, we have become externally focused and forgotten our roots and our lineage, which stem back to the Earth...and even further to the Cosmos.

Moving away from the land of our birth, or the land of our ancestors, breaks the link to the very land we are rooted in. The more we move, the fewer roots we have. Indigenous people know this as so many were forced to move from their ancestral lands. Without our ancestral stories and rootedness to the land, we often feel like orphans, even when we have a loving family.

Disconnection to our Earth has had profound repercussions. Ultimately, we cannot live like this. It is a spiritual disease that will result in disaster for our species. The ancestors, such as those in this story, are pressing us to listen and right the situation. The solution will not be found by adding more mental constructs. We cannot think or act our way out of this safely. We can only take the deep journey of self-discovery that involves our entire life.

10 Ways to Contact and Work with Our Ancestors

Ancestors support us to correct negative patterns and wounds for ourselves, our descendants and our ancestors. We are PERFECT for the task. It's important to realize this truth or we might feel overwhelmed with feelings of inadequacy and responsibility. Our ancestors also desire to reveal our gifts and strengthen us so that we become the authentic, empowered person we are and, by working with them, we can discover this.

Here are some ways to contact and work with the ancestors:

1. **The first step is to believe.** Belief is critical, as doing so immediately strengthens their connection with you. One of the gifts of Indigenous peoples is their deep-seated belief in the existence and importance of their ancestors in their everyday lives. Belief is more difficult for our western minds, as few of us are raised with these teachings. Believing in other unseen beings, such as angels, elementals, spirits, God, the Divine Mother or Christ, can help you make the transition to believing

in ancestors. These beings, like ancestors, exist in realms made up of various frequencies of thoughts and feelings. As humans in physical bodies, it is easier to communicate with those unseen beings who are closer to our own frequency. Our own physical ancestors are a good starting point.

2. **Create an altar.** You can place images, photographs, artwork, flowers, sacred objects, crystals, or stones from your ancestral land or that of your spiritual ancestors on an altar. This becomes a special place to focus your attention on ancestors and your connection strengthens if you pray and meditate to them in that place. Visiting the land of our physical or spiritual ancestors is another way to establish connections. Your ancestors may call you to visit a country with no obvious links to your physical ancestors (such as Hawaii for me). When you do, you will likely discover a spiritual link to that land.

3. **Celebrate and re-enact rituals.** These may vary according to your ancestral lineage. For example, Christmas, Hanukah, traditional foods, and Celtic sacred days can be important times to contact ancestors. Also tell stories in your family about your dead parents, grandparents, such as what they did, where they lived, and what their struggles and gifts were. Studies have shown that the more we hear stories of the ups and downs, successes and failures, the "oscillating narrative" in our family, the better adjusted we are. If you have objects from your ancestors, share them, along with photos, especially during family events. The more often people in your lineage share a story, the stronger its connection for all of you to your ancestors.

4. **Pay attention to your dreams.** One of the first ways ancestors may contact you is in dreams, so it is important to remember

your dreams and analyze their meaning. There are herbs to assist with this, but I find it easiest to lie completely still when I awaken in the morning, or during the night, and attempt to remember the last thing in my dream and then work back until I remember the entire dream. Then write the dream in a journal and attempt to understand what it means. It is helpful to tell your dream to someone, since it makes it more present. Often more clues to the meaning are revealed by doing so. You can also write a poem, song, or make a piece of art about your dream. Some dreams deal with your daily life, whereas others are messages from your ancestors.

5. **Meditate.** Meditation builds a bridge to your ancestors as it helps raise your frequency and gives you access to the astral world where the ancestors exist. Ask Spirit to help you. Then get out of the way so Spirit can work its magic in whatever form it takes. Speak directly with the ancestors and ask them to reveal themselves—or just witness how they are working with you by the recurring fractals (patterns) in your life. Ancestors love to be recognized and appreciated, so remember to send them an open-hearted "thank you".

6. **Start where you are now!** What recurring problems do you face in your life? Look at your family history. Are your issues common to your alive or deceased relatives? Examine your health concerns, financial issues, relationships, career paths, even places you want to live. What do you notice? It is generally easier to start your ancestral journey with your family. But, if you don't find obvious connections, explore your past lives. Do this through meditation or by seeking a past life regression therapist. It is an easy procedure that provides many benefits.

7. **Forgiveness.** If you discover something about your ancestral lineage that is negative in your eyes, forgiveness is key. What you find may not be comfortable, in fact, it could be distressing. But we often find a gift within the very thing that is causing us distress. You may find a strength you did not know you had or develop a quality, such as compassion, that you were lacking. Remain in neutral, no matter what you learn, and know it is time to discover these things about yourself and/or your lineages. Why? So you can forgive yourself and your ancestors. Forgiveness removes the wound—for them and you—through all generations. On the positive side, recognizing an inner strength in an ancestor can be a tremendous gift to you and your entire lineage.

8. **Enjoy the journey of unraveling.** When you engage in the process of connecting with your ancestors, you discover that ancestors occur in many different realms and have many different messages for you...and somehow, it all has a sense of rightness. You, like me, might be surprised to discover things about yourself you never suspected as you are taken to places, both internal and external, you did not know you would ever visit. The best revelations often occur in completely unknown territory, where you cannot rely on your habitual responses.

9. **Be patient with yourself.** This process is more one of allowing than doing. Keep in mind that ancestors exist in a realm where time, as we know it, does not exist and that they perceive energetically how you are progressing with their revelations and requests. Know that they give exactly the amount you can deal with at any one time to succeed with your tasks. If you feel

overwhelmed, seek professional help. In fact, sometimes that is exactly what our ancestors wish us to do, so they nudge us in that direction.

10. **Take action in the world.** Ask yourself, "What can I best contribute to others and the world?" The answer may be something to clean up your physical, economic, or social environment. Remember that your journey is not only for you. Healing ancestral wounds affects your life, the lives of those who came before you, the lives of your descendants, and ultimately the world…in all dimensions.

Western Versus
Indigenous Thinking

To communicate with our ancestors, it can be helpful to learn and practice tried and true ways that Indigenous peoples have practiced for millennia. Ultimately, to be a fully functional creator on this planet, we need to realize that the qualities stated here under "Indigenous Mind" are actually a higher, not lower, state of consciousness.

Western Mind	Hawaiian/Indigenous Mind
Physical environment to be conquered and used	Land is sacred
Nature is passive	Nature is interactive with humans
Individual identity supreme	Interconnection with all beings
Obstacles are problems	Obstacles are tests
Independence	Interdependence
Time is linear: past, present, future	All is present now

... continued on next page

Doing is most important	Being is most important
Subject/object relationships	Embracing the whole of existence
Material world	Spirit infuses all dimensions
Either/or thinking	Both/and thinking
Mind thinking	Heart feeling
Fit into cultural, religious systems	Acquire wisdom in your unique way
Mental learning	Experiential learning
Fact focused	Mindfulness in present
Desire to control and acquire	Sense of awe and wonder
Only respect humans	Respect all beings

At a Glance

1. The goal for each of us is to become a conscious human, fully awake to all realms of existence.

2. Have faith that you are on the path and trust the unfolding process.

3. Become aware of the hunches and synchronicities in your life and know that the ancestors are helping you.

4. As you pay attention to their messages and ACT on them, these nudges increase.

5. Enter partnership with the ancestors—a sacred bond of healing—not only for yourself and those in your lineage, but ultimately for the collective unconscious of humanity.

6. You are set up to succeed.

7. Your commitment to take one step sets you on the path.

8. The ancestors watch and root for you, but only you can do the work in this third-dimensional reality called Life.

9. Enjoy the journey. It is precious. It is a path of heart and love.

10. You will find many kind souls that help you along the way and kin you never knew existed. Ancestors may contact you in many diverse ways. You may see, hear, or feel what they wish to convey.

11. Any way you receive them is your way. Discover your way.

Acknowledgements

I am keenly aware that I am a beginner in Hawaiian culture. Although this story is a true account of everything I experienced and learned in Hawaii, I believe the ancestors chose me to write it because of the universal importance of the topic of ancestors, not only for Hawaiians, but for all of us. With deep humility given this task, I can only say that any mistakes in Hawaiian words or usage (should they occur) are wholly mine.

I am deeply indebted to many Hawaiians who trusted me to share their sacred wisdom. To Serge Kahili King, who has taught huna wisdom for five decades, for his generous help; to my friend and brother on the path, Kimokeo Kapahulehua, who serves the moʻo and the ancestors; to Kale Hua, ranger and guardian at Puʻuhonua o Honaunau on the Big Island; and to Danny Hoshimoto of Kauaiquest.com who guided me to many sacred sites to meet the ancestors. Lastly, I thank Jeanne Russell and Ann Marie Holmes who invited me to Kauai and introduced me to the ʻaina (land).

Thank you to Nita Kay Alvarez for her ongoing dragon-eye editing and her helpful additions of maps and diagrams, to Janet

Rouss for an inspiring design, and to Merle Dulmadge, Jenny Linley, Werner Braun, and Sonya Roy for suggesting improvements. Honor Griffith's conversation with me about ancestors helped make sense of my experiences. I am also grateful to Monika Bernegg for her detailed proof-reading and for translating the book into German, not once but several times until I stopped my continual edits, and to Andreas Lentz and staff of NeueErde who made me look deeper to answer my unasked questions.

Mostly though, I want to thank Spirit and the ancestral challenges and heart opening opportunities I was given over a four-year period following my Hawaiian encounters. This time gifted me with the personal experiences without which this book would have lacked the essence of 'aloha'.

I am especially appreciative of Simon Goede, who encourages me and allows time during our holidays for magical interventions.

Glossary of Hawaiian Words

'aina	land, earth
ali'i	the ruling class and both males and females ruled, noble, chief
aloha	love, affection, compassion, sympathy, grace, greeting
'aumakua	ancestral guardians of family groups
'awa	the root of the kava plant prepared by chewing or pounding creates a narcotic drink for relaxation; in ceremony used as an offering to the gods
'ehu	red-haired or red-skinned people (for Hawaiians only) considered special
Els	(not a Hawaiian word) came from Sirius in very early times to help the Earth condense and make more water and land
hā	the divine breath of life
haole	foreigner, usually white European
honi	traditional Hawaiian greeting where you press your noses and foreheads together while gazing into each other's eyes and share the hā (breath)
heiau	an ancient Hawaiian temple
hula	traditional dance of Hawaii
huna	something indefinite; esoteric knowledge
hune	little person; someone poor in Tahitian

kahiki	Tahitian word means to transform; in Hawaiian, there were five kahikis of ascending levels until you are in outer space
kahuna	male or female priest, sorcerer, magician, shaman
kāhuna	plural
King Kamehameha the Great	conquered all the Hawaiian Islands
kakau	tattoo
kapu	taboo, sacred, prohibited, forbidden, no trespassing
konane	a game resembling checkers
kikokilo	a kind of kahuna that predicts future events
koʻokoʻo	a carved walking stick
kuhikuhi puʻuone	a kind of kahuna that locate building sites for temples
kumu	teacher, model, expert in an area
kupuna	wise elder, the senior representative of the living past, physically and/or spiritually
Laka	goddess of the wild woods, patroness of all vegetation, and of hula
lapaʻau	a kind of kahuna that is a healer
lei	garland, necklace of flowers, leaves, shells, ivory, feathers, given as a symbol of affection
loko ia	this pond
mana	life force, to have power, authority
mano	commonly means shark in Hawaiian; a generic word for animals that have teeth, swim in the surf, have a high dorsal fin, and give live birth; includes dolphins
manahune	Tahitian word means people of the secret power because *mana* means power
menehune	Legendary race of small people who worked at night, building fish ponds, roads, temples

mo'o are 'aumakua	ancestral gods who protect descendants from danger or sorcery, heal sickness or wounds, and forgive transgressions; guardians of water, rivers, ponds, and freshwater sources; gecko-like shapeshifters that can appear in form of a 12 to 30-foot-long water dragon
mo'okane	another name for mo'o that wear human-like bodies combined with lizard features; guardians of the Earth related to the creator god Kane
mo'oku'auhau	genealogy describes the interlocking bones of the spine of the mo'o
mo'olelo	a progression of words like the mo'o spine
muumuu	Hawaiian short-sleeved, round-yoked dress in varying lengths
namu	a race of beings, the word means the silent ones
nawa	the noisy ones, referring to menehune
nawao	giants that were always found in the wilderness
'ohana	family, kin group, can mean community of hula dancers, good friends
'ohia lehua/'ohelo	red puff-ball shaped flowers; legend says pluck and it will rain.
Pele	Volcano goddess and fire is one of her aspects
prana	Vedic/Hindu word, meaning life force energy. Mana is the Hawaiian equivalent
peke /epa'a	spirits with diverse characteristics
Tuatha de Danaan	an old race originating in Lemurian times; ancestors of elementals
wahine	woman, female
Waitaha	original race of beings living in New Zealand prior to the Maori; includes Polynesians, fairy beings, Orientals. There is no Hawaiian equivalent
wao	wilderness

Further Reading

Duprée, Ulrich E. *Ho'oponopono and Family Constellations: A traditional Hawaiian healing method for relationships, forgiveness and love*, Earthdancer Books, 2017.

Easter, Sandra, *Jung and the Ancestors*, London, Muswell Hill Press, 2016.

Farmer, Steven, *Healing Ancestral Karma*, San Antonio, TX: Hierophant Publishing, 2014.

Furlong, David, *Healing Your Ancestral Patterns*, Malvern, Worchestershire: Atlanta Books, 2014.

Grimassi, Raven, *Communing with the Ancestors*, Newburyport, MA: Weiser, 2016.

Hollis, James, *Hauntings*, Asheville, NC: Chiron Publications, 2013.

Hintze, R. *Healing Your Family History*, Carlesbad, CA: Hay House, 2006.

Jacobs, A. J., *It's All Relative: Adventures up and down the World's Family Tree*, New York, Simon and Schuster, 2017.

King, Serge Kahili, *Huna, Ancient Hawaiian Secrets for Modern Living*. New York, Atria Books, 2008.

Lipton, Bruce, *Biology of Belief*, Hay House, CA: 2007.

O'Sullivan and Graydon, *The Ancestral Continuum*, New York, Atria Books, 2013.

Sykes, Bryan, *The Seven Daughters of Eve*, New York, W.W. Norton & Co., 2001.

Thomas, Ariann, *Healing Family Patterns*, 2011.

Wesselman, Hank, *The Bowl of Light*, Boulder, CO: Sounds True, 2011.

Additional Resources

Ancestry.com, Wikitree.com, Familysearch.org
for genealogy and DNA testing.

National Geographic Geno-2 for DNA testing.

About the Author

Tanis Helliwell, M.Ed. is the founder of the International Institute for Transformation. Since January, 2000, IIT has offered programs to assist individuals in becoming conscious creators to work with the spiritual laws that govern our world. Tanis, a mystic in the modern world, has brought spiritual consciousness into the mainstream for over three decades.

She is the author of *Summer with the Leprechauns, Pilgrimage with the Leprechauns, Decoding Your Destiny, Manifest Your Soul's Purpose, Embraced by Love, Take Your Soul to Work* and *Hybrids.* Her DVDs, *Elementals and Nature Spirits, Hybrids and Spiritual Transformation,* as well as her *Personal Growth, Inner Mysteries and Self-Healing* CDs, are helpful to individuals who want to work with elementals and other sentient beings evolving on Earth.

She is a student and teacher of the Inner Mysteries, living on the seacoast north of Vancouver, Canada. Since childhood, she has seen and heard elementals, angels, and master teachers in higher dimensions. Tanis conducted a psychotherapy practice for 30 years, helping individuals with their spiritual transformation. To heal the Earth and catalyze individual transformation, she led tours and walking pilgrimages to sacred sites around the world for over 20 years, while serving as an international management consultant to create healthy government, corporate and health care organizations.

Tanis Helliwell is a sought-after keynote speaker whose insightful awareness is applied in a variety of spiritual disciplines. She has presented at conferences featuring Rupert Sheldrake, Matthew Fox, Barbara Marx Hubbard, Gregg Braden, Fritjof Capra, and Jean Houston. These conferences include The Science and Consciousness Conference in Albuquerque, The World Future Society in Washington, D.C., and Spirit and Business conferences in Boston, Toronto, Vancouver, and Mexico City. Tanis has also presented at Findhorn, Hollyhock, A.R.E. Edgar Cayce, Alice Bailey and Anthroposophical conferences.

Tanis works a great deal in Europe and with psychiatrists, medical practitioners, and other healers to clear the etheric and astral bodies in developing healthy consciousness.

To write to the author for information on upcoming workshops, please contact:

Tanis Helliwell
1766 Hollingsworth Rd.,
Powell River, BC., Canada V8A 0M4

E-mail: tanis@tanishelliwell.com
Web sites: www.tanishelliwell.com/ www.iitransform.com
www.facebook.com/Tanis.Helliwell

BOOKS:

- *Hybrids: So you think you are human*
- *Summer with the Leprechauns: the authorized edition*
- *Pilgrimage with the Leprechauns: a true story of a mystical tour of Ireland*
- *Decoding Your Destiny: keys to humanity's spiritual transformation*
- *Manifest Your Soul's Purpose*
- *Take Your Soul to Work*
- *Embraced by Love*

DVDs

1. Elementals and Nature Spirits
2. Hybrids: So you think you are human
3. Spiritual Transformation: Journey of Co-creation

CDs

Series A — *Personal Growth Collection: Two Visualizations*

1. Path of Your Life / Your Favorite Place
2. Eliminating Negativity / Purpose of Your Life
3. Linking Up World Servers / Healing the Earth

Series B — *Inner Mysteries Collection: Talk and Visualization*

1. The Celtic Mysteries / Quest for the Holy Grail
2. The Egyptian Mysteries / Initiation in the Pyramid of Giza
3. The Greek Mysteries / Your Male and Female Archetypes
4. The Christian Mysteries / Jesus' Life: A Story of Initiation
5. Address from The Earth/ Manifesting Peace on Earth

Series C – *The Self-Healing Series: Talk and Visualization*

1. The Body Elemental / Healing with the Body Elemental
2. Rise of the Unconscious / Encountering Your Shadow
3. Reawakening Ancestral Memory / Between the Worlds

CPSIA information can be obtained
at www.ICGtesting.com
Printed in the USA
FSHW021842100419
57136FS